RIP VAN WINKLE, OR "THE WORKS"

Richard Nelson

BROADWAY PLAY PUBLISHING INC
224 E 62nd St, NY, NY 10065
www.broadwayplaypub.com
info@broadwayplaypub.com

RIP VAN WINKLE, OR "THE WORKS"
© Copyright 1982, 1986 by Richard Nelson

All rights reserved. This work is fully protected under the copyright laws of the United States of America. No part of this publication may be photocopied, reproduced, stored in a retrieval system, or transmitted, in any form or by any means, electronic, mechanical, recording, or otherwise, without the prior permission of the publisher. Additional copies of this play are available from the publisher.

Written permission is required for live performance of any sort. This includes readings, cuttings, scenes, and excerpts. For amateur and stock performances, please contact Broadway Play Publishing Inc. For all other rights please contact the author c/o B P P I.

Cover art compliments of Yale Repertory Theater

First published by B P P I in December 1986

I S B N: 978-0-88145-694-3

First printing: November 2016

Book design: Marie Donovan
Typographic controls: Adobe InDesign
Typeface: Palatino
Printed and bound in the U S A

for David Jones

RIP VAN WINKLE, OR "THE WORKS" premiered at the Yale Repertory Theater (Lloyd Richards, Artistic Director) on 4 December 1981. The cast and creative contributors were:

RIP VAN WINKLE	Seth Allen
GRETCHEN	Laura Esterman
MEENIE *(girl)*	Patricia McGuire
MEENIE *(woman)*	Kaiulani Lee
HANS DERRICK	Gerry Bamman
COCKLES	Alan Rosenberg
HEINRICH VEDDER *(boy)*	Jon Walker
HEINRICH VEDDER *(man)*	Stephen Lang

PART ONE

FOREMAN	John E Harnagel
FIRST WORKER	Kevin McClarnon
SECOND WORKER	Dan Desmond
AUNTIE	Mary Van Dyke
SURVEYOR	Vic Polizos
SOLDIER	Steven Ryan
REV JOHNSON	Richard Jamieson
MRS JOHNSON	Jane Kaczmarek
NICK VEDDER	Baxter Harris
HUDSON GHOST	Michael Grodenchik

PART TWO

HENRY	Richard Jamieson
FRANCIS	Steven Ryan
JACK	Vic Polizos
BOY	Jon Walker

SECRETARY	Dan Desmond
HOUSEKEEPER	Zakiah Barksdale
SERVANT GIRL	Becky London
MAN ON PUMP	Michael Grodenchik
MAN WITH BUCKETS	Baxter Harris
BURNING MAN	Kevin McClarnon
CONSTABLE	John Lloyd
GUARD	Charles S Dutton
SGT JONES	Baxter Harris
LOOKOUT	Kevin Mcclarnon
CORPORAL	Michael Grodenchik
SCHOOLTEACHER	Warren David Keith

PART THREE

CLYDE	Charles S Dutton
EDWARD	Warren David Keith
RICHARD	John Lloyd
JONATHAN	Steven Ryan
JUDITH	Mary Van Dyke
DUTCH	Kevin McClarnon
GEORGE	Michael Grodenchik
SHEPHERD	Frank Maraden
SHEPHERD'S BROTHER	Vic Polizos
LAWYER	Baxter Harris
POSTMASTER	Richard Jamieson
PAUL	Dan Desmond
SAM	John E Harnagel
Director	David Jones
Set design	Douglas O Stein
Costume design	Gene K Lakin
Lighting design	Jennifer Tipton

PART ONE
"DRUNK"

Scene One

(Near a muddy road. Morning. FOREMAN *and* FIRST WORKER *look off. Noise of wagons, shouts, horses)*

FOREMAN: Help him!

VOICE: Stuck!

FIRST WORKER: Stuck.

FOREMAN: Help him!

FIRST WORKER: Get his face. Pull!

FOREMAN: Pull! Pull! Goddamn mud.

FIRST WORKER: *(To himself)* Pull. Please. Pull. Pull.

FOREMAN: Get to him! That's a man! A man!

FIRST WORKER: *(Under his breath)* Flesh and blood. They can't get close.

FOREMAN: The head! Get his head!

FIRST WORKER: They can't stand up. He's choking.

FOREMAN: By the hair then!

FIRST WORKER: The mud. Gonna drown.

FOREMAN: Stupid. It's just stupid!

FIRST WORKER: Mud.

(Horse screams off.)

FOREMAN: Now what?

VOICE: Stuck!

FOREMAN: What the hell is that horse stopped for?!! Move it!

FIRST WORKER: Stuck. He's gonna drown. Pull. Pull.

FOREMAN: Move that horse!

FIRST WORKER: Reach him. Please.

FOREMAN: You don't move it we're going to have two hundred stuck horses!

VOICE: Stuck!

FOREMAN: Unstuck it! Oh, Christ, it's down.

VOICE: Help! I need help!

FOREMAN: It's down. No. No.

FIRST WORKER: They reached him.

FOREMAN: No get it back up! Come on. Please. Please. Please.

VOICE: Stuck!

FOREMAN: Then shoot it! Either get that horse up or shoot it!

FIRST WORKER: Out. He's out. The mud.

(Gun shot off)

FIRST WORKER: They shot it.

(Horse screams.)

FOREMAN: Wounded. Don't believe this. Wounded. Stupid. In the head! Not in the back!

(SECOND WORKER *struggles in, coughing, covered with mud, exhausted.)*

FOREMAN: Stupid!!

(Horse screams.)

PART ONE

FIRST WORKER: Dying.

FOREMAN: I don't want it dying, I want it dead! Shoot it! *(Runs out)*

SECOND WORKER: Water.

FIRST WORKER: *(Points)* There's a stream.

(SECOND WORKER nods.)

FIRST WORKER: Here. *(Offers his hand; helps him up.)*

SECOND WORKER: Slippery. Fell down. Wouldn't let go.

FIRST WORKER: What wouldn't?

SECOND WORKER: The mud. *(Starts to leave; stops)* Didn't know a man could drown in mud, did you? *(No response)* Well, now you know.

(Horse screams in pain.)

FOREMAN: *(Off)* Shoot!!!!!!

Scene Two

(Edge of a stream. Large rock. GRETCHEN and AUNTIE scrub clothes. MEENIE, a young girl, sits, she stares off right. Far upstage a SURVEYOR with tripod. He surveys off left.)

MEENIE: So many wagons! Mother, what comes after twelve?

(Short pause; GRETCHEN ignores her.)

MEENIE: Thirteen comes after twelve, doesn't it? Twelve. Thirteen. Fourteen. Fifteen. Seventeen. Mother, I never saw so many wagons before in my whole life! Have you, Mother?

(GRETCHEN ignores her.)

MEENIE: Seventeen wagons going to the works. I wonder what's in all those wagons, Mother? Do you know? Do you have any idea? Oh there's my favorite!

That one there with the six mules! That's the prettiest of them all, don't you think so! *(Short pause)* Mother, which one is Father driving? I'll bet it's that one with the mules. I'll bet that's the one, don't you?

(GRETCHEN *just continues working.*)

AUNTIE: Meenie, why don't you go and get a little closer. Maybe then you can see your father. But don't get too close. And stay out of everyone's way. And don't go getting that dress dirty. And…

MEENIE: *(Almost off)* Can I, Mother? Can I?!

AUNTIE: Go.

(MEENIE *runs out. Pause. They scrub.*)

AUNTIE: So you don't talk to your own daughter anymore?

GRETCHEN: And say what?

AUNTIE: She's your daughter.

GRETCHEN: *(Shouts)* And say what?!!!

AUNTIE: Relax. Relax.

GRETCHEN: That her father is a drunkard?

AUNTIE: You don't have to say a word about him, if you don't…

GRETCHEN: That if it weren't for my working myself half to death we'd all of us be starving? That every time he has so much as a penny in his pocket it ends up being poured down his throat? Or his so-called pals' throats?

AUNTIE: Gretchen…

GRETCHEN: That all we got left in this world after all his father left him is one shed that my mother left me, and that he'd have drunk that too if I hadn't kept it in my name? That her father didn't come home last night, and that I'd bet my soul he isn't on one of those

PART ONE

wagons but passed out under some tree—even though it's the first bit of real work he's got in years? That my daughter's got a father who's got a wife who is not only worn down, but pretty nearly worn out from trying to reform him and trying to convince herself that he still can be reformed? Is that what I tell her? Is it?

AUNTIE: No.

GRETCHEN: Then right now I have nothing else to say to anyone. *(Looks at some clothes)* Beer stains. How I'd give anything to clean dirt for a change.

AUNTIE: You take things too much to heart.

GRETCHEN: I have to go to work.

(They start to pick up the clothes; MEENIE runs in; SURVEYOR exits with tripod.)

MEENIE: I couldn't see him, Mother. I could see all the drivers, but I couldn't see him. Maybe he's coming later with a bigger wagon. Maybe he's coming with eight mules!

GRETCHEN: Maybe.

(They start to leave; gunshot in the distance; horse screaming.)

AUNTIE: What's…?

MEENIE: Look, it's a horse! They're shooting a horse!

AUNTIE: Let's go, Meenie. Come along.

MEENIE: But why would they shoot a horse?! Look, he's…!

AUNTIE: Don't look. Come here. Don't look.

MEENIE: But…!

GRETCHEN: Why shouldn't she, she sees more suffering every day of the week in her own home. *(She exits.)*

MEENIE: *(Crying)* Mother! Stop them!

AUNTIE: *(Holding* MEENIE*)* Did I ever tell you the story about the horse who died and then turned into a Prince?

MEENIE: I'm too old for fairy tales.

AUNTIE: Then I'll just tell it to myself. Once upon a time there was a handsome prince....

MEENIE: But the horse!

AUNTIE: You hold your horses and I'll get to him. First—the prince.

(They have exited. A SOLDIER *enters. He is wet, carries some of his clothes.)*

SOLDIER: Where'd he go now? Peter! Peter! I saw him just a minute ago. Peter!!

VOICE: *(From behind the rock)* Ahhhhhhhh!

(SOLDIER *is startled, grabs his rifle.* RIP *appears from behind the rock, holding his head.)*

RIP: Put that thing down. What did you think I was, an Indian? Well, then you'd be a damned fool 'cause there ain't no Indians around here no more. Though I wish there was, 'cause Indians know how to whisper. They know how to respect a man's sleep. They wear moccasins. You got anything to drink?

SOLDIER: The stream. *(Calls)* Peter!!

RIP: Ah! What's that? Thunder?

SOLDIER: Huh?

RIP: Nah, must be in the head. Yeh, there it is again. Sure sounds like thunder though. *(Sitting down)* Oh where are the birds? Where are the crickets chirping? This town's getting too crowded for me.

SOLDIER: You seen a surveyor around here?

PART ONE

RIP: If he was up in the clouds I might have seen him, 'cause that's where my head was pointed. But my eyes, they were closed. How about a drink?

SOLDIER: Got nothing.

RIP: Me too. I swore off.

SOLDIER: Must have thought I got lost. Told him I'd be a minute, that was half an hour ago. Went to take a bath, left my clothes on the bank, then two women and a kid come by. Have to hide in the trees 'til they go. Even though I'm travelling I still keep my pride.

RIP: Pride. That's a good thing to keep. I got mine somewhere here. *(Checks his pockets)*

SOLDIER: *(Looking)* Is that him? Peter! ...No.

RIP: You want to know what I think?

SOLDIER: No.

RIP: I think your friend, he strolls down to the inn, he props his feet up on the table, and he has himself a morning beer. A nice cool morning beer. That's the best beer of the day.

SOLDIER: The morning beer.

RIP: Or the best beer of the early part of the day.

SOLDIER: Of the morning.

RIP: Exactly.

SOLDIER: The morning beer's the best beer of the morning.

RIP: No doubt about it. That's what I think, and you can have that thought for free. See, that's how we are around here—generous. We help each other out; watch each others' kids; look after each other when we're sick; buy each other drinks.

SOLDIER: Here he comes. Peter! *(Takes out a bottle and drinks)* Peter!

(RIP *clears his throat.*)

RIP: Thought you had nothing?

SOLDIER: (*Puts bottle away*) Don't. I swore off.

SURVEYOR: (*Entering*) Where the hell you been?

RIP: Naked and in the bushes.

SOLDIER: It's a long story. See, these women…

RIP: Ah! Women! It's always women, isn't it?

SOLDIER: I…

SURVEYOR: Who's he?

RIP: A thirsty man.

SOLDIER: Peter, wait, it's not what you….

SURVEYOR: Forget it, I don't have time. You find anything out?

SOLDIER: Not yet, but…

SURVEYOR: Right. Too busy running around in the bushes…

RIP: Naked.

SOLDIER: I…

RIP: With women!

SOLDIER: (*Yells*) Who asked you????

RIP: Just trying to be helpful. See, that's how we are around here—helpful. Watch each others' kids; look after each other when we're sick; buy each other drinks.

SURVEYOR: (*Has taken out a bottle and a map*) Here!

(*Throws* RIP *the bottle.*)

RIP: Ahhh! Dawn is breaking.

SURVEYOR: (*To* SOLDIER) We ought to make friends with the natives. (*Looks over the map*)

PART ONE

RIP: *(Takes a drink)* A new day has begun! Ahhh!

SURVEYOR: This *(The map)* is a piece of crap. Seen better maps of Heaven than this of this county. I got about eighteen acres sketched in so far. Put on your clothes, we still have a lot of work left to do.

RIP: *(Drinking)* Let there be light *(To* SOLDIER*)* Nice man. Drink?

(SOLDIER *stares at* RIP.)

RIP: Oh that's right, you swore off.

SOLDIER: You want help or should I go into town?

SURVEYOR: First, the land. I want to walk the hills to the north, they could be strategic.

SOLDIER: Fine by me.

SURVEYOR: Later we can both go and look up this Mister Rip Van Winkle.

SOLDIER: Whatever you say.

RIP: *(He chokes; quietly.)* Who?

SURVEYOR: What he say?

SOLDIER: "Who?"

SURVEYOR: Him.

SOLDIER: No, that's what he said—"Who?"

SURVEYOR: Who what?

RIP: Who did you say you were going to look up?

SURVEYOR: Mister Rip Van Winkle. Why?

RIP: No no no reason. Just... You know. I heard you say and... Are you from the works?

SOLDIER: What's he talking about?

SURVEYOR: The works. They're building some works down the way. Saw the wagons.

SOLDIER: No, we are not from the works. We're from Boston. We are part of an army.

RIP: Ah.

SOLDIER: Come on, we got work to do.

SURVEYOR: Wait. Maybe he knows him.

RIP: Me? Do I...Rip Van Winkle? Uh, well, I guess you could say, he's sort of a friend of mine. Close friend. Very very close. You've never met him?

SURVEYOR: No.

SOLDIER: Never.

RIP: I see. What exactly do you want with good ol' Rip? If I may ask.

SURVEYOR: Show him the map.

(SOLDIER *does.*)

RIP: Of course it's none of my business.

SOLDIER: This is the most recent we could come up with. Twenty years old.

RIP: *(Looking)* Ah.

SOLDIER: *(Pointing)* Look at that.

RIP: Ah.

SOLDIER: And there.

RIP: Ah.

SOLDIER: And there.

RIP: Ah.

SOLDIER: And this area here.

RIP: Ah.

SOLDIER: You see what we mean now?

RIP: Ah. I don't read.

PART ONE

SURVEYOR: *(Pushes* SOLDIER *away)* What we're trying to show you is that each of these large plots are labeled as being owned by a certain Rip Van Winkle. And, as it's part of our task at this point to gain the support of the more wealthy gentlemen of the community, we are, as you can understand, rather anxious to meet up with this Mister Van Winkle.

RIP: I see. Hmmmmmm. *(Takes a drink)* And you really don't…? Not even the color of his hair?

SURVEYOR: He's a name on a map.

RIP: Interesting. Excuse me. *(Drinks)* He's a busy man.

SURVEYOR: Our business won't take long.

RIP: I guess in that case…after all, who am I to deny you such a pleasure.

SOLDIER: Mister Van Winkle?

RIP: He… is there any more?

(SURVEYOR *nudges* SOLDIER *to give* RIP *his bottle.*)

RIP: Thank you. *(Drinks)* Mmmmmmmm.

SOLDIER: You were saying?

RIP: Saying? What was I saying? Oh right. I believe with my whole heart that no more true or decent, no kinder man has ever breathed God's air, than Mister Van Winkle. *(Drinks)* Ahhhh. Of course, I can only really speak for myself, but for myself this I can swear—I would not be alive today, if it weren't for Rip Van Winkle. I would not be here, or there, or anywhere for that matter. In fact, I would have no breath at all, if it were not for….

(HEINRICH, *a boy, runs in.)*

HEINRICH: There you are. Mister Derrick sent me looking for you.

(RIP *shushes* HEINRICH *and winks.)*

HEINRICH: What? He said you never showed for work, and that if I was to find you, and you weren't dead or almost dead then you'll never get to drive no wagon for him.

RIP: *(To men)* Rip Van Winkle will give me work. I have nothing to worry about.

HEINRICH: Huh? What are you talking about, Rip...?

RIP: Van Winkle. That's just who we're talking about. Sh-sh!

SOLDIER: *(To* SURVEYOR*)* Derrick.

SURVEYOR: Who?

SOLDIER: Derrick. The letter. That rider at the inn in Pittsfield gave us a letter for a Mister Derrick. *(To* RIP*)* Gave us two shillings to deliver it.

RIP: Come along gentlemen, I know a comfortable little inn which, besides its obvious charm, is often visited by Mister Van Winkle. Come. Come.

(They start to go. SECOND WORKER *enters, still covered in mud, on his way to the stream.)*

SOLDIER: God, what happened to him?

SECOND WORKER: Fell in the mud.

RIP: Come on, come on. Let's not dawdle.

SECOND WORKER: What's the hurry? Got a couple of suckers to buy you a drink, Rip?

(Pause)

SURVEYOR: Rip?

SOLDIER: Rip?

RIP: Rip? Rip? What's ripped? Did something rip? *(Pause; he looks up at the sky.)* Going to rain. *(Pause; then he puts on a big toothy innocent smile.)* Do you want your bottle back?

Scene Three

(Beer garden. Tables. Late morning. REV JOHNSON, MRS JOHNSON, *and* COCKLES *[*DERRICK's *nephew] stand, looking out a telescope toward the works.* DERRICK *sits and watches them.)*

REV JOHNSON: *(Looking)* Mmmmmm. How wonderfully inspirational to witness a beginning. The effort alone fills one with hope.

DERRICK: Yes.

REV JOHNSON: God bless you, sir, and He thanks you. You are making our work all the easier.

COCKLES: How so?

REV JOHNSON: My flock, it appears, shall be quite exhausted by Sunday. And tired muscles cannot the Lord resist.

DERRICK: And what do you think, Mrs Johnson?

(She slowly goes to the telescope and looks through.)

MRS JOHNSON: *(Finally; quietly, without conviction)* It's lovely.

REV JOHNSON: *(Laughs)* Lovely!

DERRICK: Very sweet. *(Laughs)*

REV JOHNSON: That's a woman for you.

DERRICK: I'm not sure "lovely" is the right word, Mrs Johnson. I think "serviceable" might be more appropriate for a works.

*(*MRS JOHNSON *tries to hold back tears.)*

MRS JOHNSON: Excuse me. *(She runs off sobbing.)*

DERRICK: I hope it was not what I said.

REV JOHNSON: I can assure you it was not, Mister Derrick. My wife is rather high strung. She has not yet learned the art of adapting.

DERRICK: I see.

REV JOHNSON: It will take time. Six months of marriage after all is nothing. One will have to work at it. And that, of course, takes time.

DERRICK: Of course.

REV JOHNSON: She is still quite young. And girls as I am sure you are aware still have their heads full of dreams. I think she was rather distraught at my not getting a more—shall we say—urban parish.

DERRICK: In time, Rev Johnson, this shall be an urban parish, if I have my way.

REV JOHNSON: You and I can see that. You and I see the house when only the foundation is built, but my wife unfortunately when she looks at your works all she sees is dirt. It is theaters and boulevards she wishes to see through your telescope.

DERRICK: Yes.

REV JOHNSON: *(Moves away from the telescope.)* If there is anything I can do, Mister Derrick, please do not refrain from calling. As you are now servicing this town, I shall strive to service you. It is my belief that God's will must be seen to on more days than just one. I am unlike most ministers, I don't mind getting dirty.... I should go and see to my wife. Trust me, she has it in her to be both charming and delightful. *(Starts to go)* Tell me something, Mister Derrick. How can a girl who has spent her entire life on a farm be so repulsed by dirt?

DERRICK: She'll change.

REV JOHNSON: *(Nods)* Theaters. She wouldn't even know how to behave in one. *(Leaves)*

DERRICK: *(Stands)* Cockles, let me see. *(Looks through the telescope)* It's lovely.

PART ONE

(HEINRICH *appears around the corner. He watches for a moment, then pretends to run in out of breath.*)

HEINRICH: I found him. *(Pants)* Just let me catch my... *(Pants)* You wouldn't believe all the places I'm looking. *(Pants)*

DERRICK: And...?

HEINRICH: And! He was just lying there, poor Rip. Seems he's on his way to the works real early this morning. Real real early and... *(Pants)* he gets kicked by this horse. It's hard to believe, but there's this horse and it kicks him right in the head. Poor Rip. And he looks up at me and he says to me, "Heinrich, help me get to work". And I says, "Rip you can't go to work today, you've been kicked in the head". And he says, "Help me up". And I says, "No, don't move, Mister Derrick he's going to understand". And he says, "But". And I says, "But". And then he's trying to stand by himself, but his legs they won't hold him up, so he looks up at me and he says, "Yes, Mister Derrick is a nice man" and then he groans. Poor Rip.

DERRICK: "Poor Rip." *(Turns away)*

(Short pause)

HEINRICH: *(Pants)* And then I start running *(Heavier panting)* and I don't stop for nothing because I know that Mister Derrick he wants to know what I know so I'm running *(Even heavier panting)* and I keep running 'til I get here. *(Very heavy panting)*

(Finally DERRICK *reaches into his pocket, gives him a coin, and* HEINRICH *stops his heavy breathing, smiles and starts to walk off.* NICK—*the owner of the Gardens and* HEINRICH's *father—has entered and grabs him.*)

NICK: *(Slaps* HEINRICH *across the face; he stutters.)* Where-wherewhere you been? He runs off for all morning. Now get inin there and get to work!

DERRICK: Your boy was doing me an errand, Nick.

NICK: *(To* HEINRICH*)* Open your hand! Open open it! *(Slaps him)* A shillilling. Now what were you going to do with a shilling?

DERRICK: I gave it to your boy, Nick. Not to you.

NICK: A boy don't need a shilling! This boy needs, he needs somethin' else. *(Grabs* HEINRICH*)*

DERRICK: Let him go.

NICK: I'm his father!

DERRICK: Don't blame the boy for that!

(GRETCHEN *has entered; she wears an apron; she counts change.)*

NICK: You shouldn't talk like that in front of my boy. It ain't right.

HEINRICH: Knock him down! Just knock him down!

NICK: IIIIII...

GRETCHEN: He can't. Or won't

DERRICK: *(Quietly)* Gretchen.

NICK: You got myyyy boy upset.

HEINRICH: *(Yells)* Knock him down!!!!!

NICK: Boy...

GRETCHEN: He can't! Because that man's got a county and a works and he's got an Inn that don't make him a pound a year. So he can't. Or won't.

(Pause)

NICK: Boy? *(He goes to* HEINRICH *and tries to rub his hair.)*

HEINRICH: Get away from me!

NICK: Whaaaaat kind of talk's that?

HEINRICH: Why didn't you knock him down?

PART ONE

NICK: You can't go knocking people down, boy, not when they're payin'. You're oooold enough to know that.

(Pause)

GRETCHEN: Go inside, Heinrich. I want to speak with your father.

(HEINRICH *slowly leaves.* NICK *starts to clean up.*)

NICK: You shouldn't have sssssaid what you said, Mister Derrick. But just toooooo show I got no bad feelings, Gretchen, geeeeeet Mister Derrick another drink.

GRETCHEN: I'm not getting nothing until you explain why you paid me one and three when you know damn well I've earned one and six.

NICK: *(Screams)* Get him a drink!!!!!!

(Pause, GRETCHEN *doesn't move.)*

NICK: I paid what I owed.

GRETCHEN: But I...

NICK: It may be less than what you earned, but it's what I owed.

GRETCHEN: Come again.

NICK: Now don't you start something, Gretchen Van Winkle. I have never cheated nobody in my life.

GRETCHEN: There's a first for everything.

NICK: I told you—I paid what I owed!

GRETCHEN: But I earned...!

NICK: But there was a bill!

GRETCHEN: A what?

NICK: A bill. That was owed me. That's all.

GRETCHEN: A bill? What kind of...? *(Stops, realizes, suddenly very upset)* When was he here?!! When?!!!!!

NICK: I couldn't refuse him, could I? Rip without something to drink—that's paththethtic. I got a big heart.

GRETCHEN: With my money!! *(She sits, holds her head, fights back tears.)* Why do I even... Why bother. God I feel so foolish. I can't remember the last time I cried. As if tears were... What a waste.

(DERRICK *tries to give* GRETCHEN *a handkerchief*)

GRETCHEN: *(Screams)* Nooooo!!

(Pause)

DERRICK: *(Motioning for* NICK *to leave)* Nick...

(NICK *starts to leave but stops.*)

GRETCHEN: *(To* DERRICK*)* You. You've sucked out his acres and now he's bone dry. Go away.

DERRICK: I paid a fair price, Gretchen.

GRETCHEN: I wouldn't know. Went down his throat and into his (NICK's) pocket. I wouldn't know. *(Slowly stands; yells)* Give me that handkerchief!!!!

(*He does; she blows her nose.*)

GRETCHEN: I don't know what's the matter with me. *(Rubs her eyes)*

(HEINRICH *has entered and watches.*)

DERRICK: *(To* NICK*)* The boy.

GRETCHEN: Let him see. Let him. Maybe then he'll think twice before he becomes a drunk like the rest of them.

(Pause)

NICK: Look, I don't want to stop a man from having a good ttiiiime.

GRETCHEN: A good time. Sure. Why not.

(NICK *exits with* HEINRICH. *Pause.*)

DERRICK: You hate him?

GRETCHEN: You'd like it if I did.

DERRICK: I wouldn't.

GRETCHEN: Funny, aren't I? Go ahead and laugh. Fifteen years ago I could have had you. But then I wanted a good time. I was a girl.... God, I try. It's that damn good humor that I just can't stand. What's to be so happy about? Sometimes I find myself just screaming at him—what's to be so happy about!

DERRICK: The boy said he got kicked by a horse. That's why he didn't show up at the works.

GRETCHEN: I wish. (*Pause. She starts to pick up things.*)

DERRICK: Gretchen...

GRETCHEN: Don't ask.

DERRICK: There's room, Gretchen. You could have a whole floor to yourself. You could be my cook. I'd pay. It's a job. Nothing more.

(*Pause*)

GRETCHEN: No. I can't change. (*She leaves.*)

COCKLES: She'll change.

(MRS JOHNSON *enters, she's very nervous, awkward.*)

MRS JOHNSON: I came back to apologize for my behavior.

DERRICK: There's no need to...

MRS JOHNSON: It must have been the heat. I am quite susceptible to heat.

DERRICK: I understand.

(MRS JOHNSON *turns;* REV JOHNSON *has entered. She turns back.)*

MRS JOHNSON: *(Holding out a book)* Have you read this?

DERRICK: I'm afraid I....

MRS JOHNSON: The characters are most exceptionally drawn. One almost gets the sense that one knows them. As if you could recognize them if they walked by... And they might recognize you and say "hello"... If you'd like to borrow it... *(She holds it out)*

DERRICK: *(Taking the book)* Thank you.

MRS JOHNSON: *(Nods)* Goodbye. *(She exits.)*

REV JOHNSON: See—charming and delightful. Good day. *(He exits; Pause.)*

DERRICK: *(To* COCKLES*)* Come on, boy, let's go to work.

(They leave. HEINRICH *enters, clearing off the tables.)*

VOICE: Psst. Pssst!

*(*RIP *enters.)*

HEINRICH: Sh-sh! *(Points to where his father is, off)*

RIP: How much did Derrick give you?

HEINRICH: Shilling.

RIP: Good work.

HEINRICH: My father took it.

RIP: That's life.

HEINRICH: You want a bottle? *(Takes out a bottle from under his shin)*

RIP: You stole it?

HEINRICH: He beat me.

RIP: Fair is fair. *(Takes the bottle, winks. He drinks. He saunters over to the telescope, looks through.)* What a lot of dirt.

Scene Four

(DERRICK's *office. Table and chair. A telescope is set up at one window.*)

(DERRICK, COCKLES, SOLDIER *and* SURVEYOR. *As the scene opens,* COCKLES *stands at a distance, the other three are pushing their chairs back and standing.*)

DERRICK: *(Holding out his hand)* Gentlemen.

SOLDIER: Mister Derrick, the armies of the Continental Congress wish to thank you.

(DERRICK *suddenly turns his head.*)

SOLDIER: What is it?

DERRICK: A fly.

(Short, awkward pause)

SURVEYOR: And I, sir, would like to add my own thanks. You must know how difficult it is to find a man with a works who's willing to sell to a rebel militia.

DERRICK: *(A bit distracted by the fly)* A man with a works can't help but be aware of the ways of His Majesty's government. The plans for these works, you know, had to be smuggled here.

SOLDIER: *(To* COCKLES*)* England doesn't want us to grow.

SURVEYOR: I have heard that of other works as well. That's why I admire your courage.

DERRICK: If I'm to keep what I own it doesn't take courage to know who has to be fought. And it's not just the English; they also have their supporters in this colony. Just west of here's a whole valley full of Canucks.

SOLDIER: Canucks, sir?

SURVEYOR: Canadians.

DERRICK: That is they still think of themselves as Canadians, though they've been south for years.

SOLDIER: Do they own a works, sir?

DERRICK: *(Shakes his head.)* Farmers.

SOLDIER: Then what do they know?

SURVEYOR: They may know how to fight.

DERRICK: I wouldn't be surprised if they had eyes on this valley as well.

SOLDIER: What do they want with two valleys?

DERRICK: Why wouldn't they?

SOLDIER: I see.

SURVEYOR: Again our thanks. You are a patriot, sir.

COCKLES: He happens to own a works.

DERRICK: Same thing. *(Swats the fly)*

COCKLES: Missed?

(DERRICK nods.)

SOLDIER: *(Pointing toward the telescope)* Would you mind?

DERRICK: *(Smiles)* No.

(SOLDIER looks through.)

COCKLES: It's delicate.

DERRICK: Tell me—what do you see?

SOLDIER: A country.

(They move to leave.)

SOLDIER: Peter, the letter.

(SURVEYOR looks at him.)

SOLDIER: The letter. From Pittsfield.

SURVEYOR: *(Begins to look through his knapsack)* Excuse us, sir. But it seems we got so caught up in recounting

PART ONE

our adventure with Van Winkle that we have left one errand uncompleted. I believe this is for you. *(Hands him the letter)* Good day.

SOLDIER: Good day.

(They leave.)

DERRICK: *(Smiles)* Cigar, boy?

COCKLES: *(Taking one)* Stupid hicks.

DERRICK: Well, I liked them. They're young. They have their vision. They have hopes. They see the broad canvas. We need each other. I, their canvas; they, someone like me to draw on it.

COCKLES: *(Turns away)* What about me?!

DERRICK: What about you???? What are you talking about? You heard what he said—a country. Well a country must have its works, and a works must have its country. I feel fifteen years younger.

COCKLES: You know they weren't any older than me, Uncle.

DERRICK: No, I guess they weren't. So what?

COCKLES: I can have a vision too!!!!

DERRICK: Who said you couldn't, boy?

COCKLES: Maybe I'm not a boy!

DERRICK: Don't be childish. Of course you're not a boy. Who said you were a boy? Look, this is just silly. *(Opens the letter that he has been fiddling with. He reads. Pause. He slams his hand on the desk.)*

COCKLES: Get it?

DERRICK: Get what?

COCKLES: *(Confused, takes the letter)* From our lawyer?

(DERRICK nods.)

COCKLES: *(Reads)* "You must obtain from Rip Van Winkle a proper conveyance for the lands you have purchased from him. The papers he has signed are in fact only loans in the form of mortgages. Hence, the lands remain his legal property; and due to the improvements on the lands, which include the works, its value is now far greater then the amount which he owes. Hence, it is within Van Winkle's legal right to sell and/or lease part or all of the lands, pay what is owed to you, and accrue a very sizable profit for himself due to the improvements you have made on his lands."

(Pause)

DERRICK: *(Quietly)* He's enclosed this deed for Van Winkle to sign.

(Long pause)

COCKLES: He'll sign. *(Short pause)* He will. *(Short pause)* Look, Uncle, I'll make him sign.

DERRICK: *(Erupts)* Use your head, boy!!!!

(FOREMAN *enters.*)

FOREMAN: Excuse me, Mister Derrick, but I've been unable to locate Van Winkle, so as you requested his wife's been told that his services will no longer be required by the Derrick Works.

DERRICK: And what was Mrs Van Winkle's reaction to this news?

FOREMAN: None. No reaction.

(DERRICK *nods, rubs his eyes.* FOREMAN *leaves.*)

DERRICK: Bugger.

COCKLES: Rip?

DERRICK: This fly… Cigar boy?

COCKLES: I have one, Uncle.

DERRICK: *(Noticing)* Ah. So do I.

(Pause. Door opens. MEENIE *appears.)*

COCKLES: I'm sorry miss—Mister Derrick is not accepting visitors.

MEENIE: *(Looks around the room.)* I. I. I. *(She starts to cry.)*

DERRICK: It's Meenie. Rip's daughter.

COCKLES: I'll get someone.

DERRICK: Yes. No. What's the matter, Meenie?

MEENIE: My fa...just because he got kicked by a... How could you?!!!! ! *(Cries)*

COCKLES: She's heard about her father.

DERRICK: Yes. To her he's still a father. Too bad she can't fire him too. So I'm a monster am I, Meenie?

MEENIE: Yes!!! *(Cries)*

DERRICK: I'm the villain, and I suppose you're the princess. And you've been terribly wronged. I understand. Everything. *(Plays with the letter; without looking at her)* How unfair it must seem. To a child's eyes. Your father. Your hope. How cruel. Everything you'd longed for, you believed was, everything you'd spent every inch of your strength to gain, it just melted. What you'd thought was stone, was ice, and you don't know what to think anymore, and the ground is moving beneath your feet, and you find yourself reaching for a cigar but you already have one....

MEENIE: What?

COCKLES: Uncle?

DERRICK: *(Screams)* I too am a princess!!!!!!!!!

COCKLES: Uncle would you like a glass of water?

DERRICK: What? *(Calm)* No. No... Meenie. I'm sorry. There's nothing I can do for your father.

(MEENIE *cries*.)

COCKLES: *(Quickly)* Except Uncle, hire him back.

DERRICK: Boy, I'm not a charity.

COCKLES: *(With much urgency)* Hire him back, Uncle! But this time not as a driver of mules.

DERRICK: Boy, she's not stupid.

COCKLES: This time, it'll be a better job. One that will take advantage of your father's talents.

DERRICK: What talents? I don't understand you, boy.

COCKLES: Your father's too intelligent a man to be a mule driver, Meenie. He was bored. That was the problem. He needed more of a challenge.

DERRICK: He's not going back to work!!

COCKLES: And we'll raise his salary. We'll double it!

DERRICK: I'm going to stop this. Foreman!

COCKLES: No, we'll triple it!

DERRICK: Triple it?!! Foreman!! Foreman!!

COCKLES: *(To* DERRICK*)* Use your head!!

DERRICK: You're out of yours. Foreman!!!!! Where is he?!!

COCKLES: But there's just one stipulation…

DERRICK: Foreman!!!!!

(FOREMAN *enters*.)

DERRICK: There you are. Would you kindly take my nephew….

COCKLES: …that your father sign a paper…

DERRICK: *(Stops)* Sign a…? *(To* FOREMAN*)* Go. Go.

COCKLES: …sign a paper…

DERRICK: Yes?

COCKLES: …stating…

DERRICK: Yes?

COCKLES: That under no circumstances will he…ever touch a drop of alcohol again. And here's the paper right here. Have him sign it. And he's hired.

(MEENIE *grabs the paper, looks first at* COCKLES *and then at* DERRICK, *who nods, then suddenly squeals with delight and runs out. Pause.* DERRICK *sits and nods.* COCKLES *goes to the telescope.*)

COCKLES: *(Looking through)* We'll let him drive the big horses. If he's drunk with them, they'll crack his skull open. *(Short pause)*

DERRICK: What do you see, Cockles?

COCKLES: *(Turns back from the telescope.)* Whatever I want to see. *(Short pause)* You didn't call me boy. *(Suddenly slaps his arm.)* Got him.

Scene Five

(Hillside. Afternoon)

(Far upstage, REV JOHNSON *and* MRS JOHNSON *are having a picnic.)*

*(*SURVEYOR *with tripod stands far left.* RIP, MEENIE *and* HEINRICH *are down stage right.* HEINRICH *holds a plumb-bob for the* SURVEYOR. RIP *drinks.)*

RIP: This place it's getting crowded. Remember when you could sit up here for a week and nobody'd bother you. Except the jackrabbits. *(Drinks)*

REV JOHNSON: Blue sky. Green hills. Cool breeze.

MRS JOHNSON: Going to rain.

SURVEYOR: God damn it, stand still!!!!

(HEINRICH *does.*)

RIP: Ahhhhh, the sun. *(Pause)* What was I talking about?

MEENIE: You were getting the rope.

RIP: The rope. What rope? Oh, the rope. I was getting the rope for my Grandmother. She was a funny lady, Meenie. I mean, she weren't funny, but I thought she was. She had a face so sharp you could chop wood with it. Never saw her face make a smile except once but that only looked like a smile, 'cause in fact she was squinting into the sun. So that's Grandmother. Anyway, the rope. So I had this piece of thin rope, and I'm tying it to two little stakes I've pounded into the ground, oh they're about eight feet apart, and the rope I tie it tight, so it's about a foot maybe off the earth. And then I'm yelling, "Grandma, Grandma!", and I'm crying, I was always crying, I was a great crier, had soft little cries, and big scratchy cries, I could play my cries like I was an instrument or something, Jesus, I was good; anyway, I'm yelling to Grandmother, and she comes out, and already I know she's not going to believe whatever it is I'm crying about, but she knows I know, but anyway she comes out and I say, "It's a chicken, it's got out of the pen", and she says, "Well get it back in the pen", and I say, 'cause I'm trying not to let her see the rope, I say, "But it flew up into the tree", and she shakes her head and spits, she loved to spit, Grandmother she spits, course nobody ever saw her spit except me, 'cause she knew nobody believed what I said so she could spit around me, and she spits and says, "Chickens don't fly into trees", and I say, "That's what I thought", and I'm pointing out what tree and she's getting closer to the rope, and that's when I realize I'm holding my breath and not crying anymore, so I start up again and I can see she can't wait to find there's no chicken up there so she can beat me and so she says something like "humpf", whatever that means, so she walks quickly toward the tree but she never gets there because she trips over the rope and falls and also I put some water there, so it's mud she falls in and that was something I wouldn't have missed for the world. She was such a funny lady, 'cause she was always doing things like that, tripping over ropes and falling into the mud. *(Laughs, drinks)* Of course, she broke her leg. And of course, I'm the one everybody wants to talk to. 'Course "talk" isn't what they mean, but that's the word they use. So Father's standing there and Mother's looking over his shoulder, and both are asking where that rope had come from to say nothing about the mud, and I'm there giving a concert of crying but sooner or later I know I got to say something, so I say, "It was a trap for the jackrabbits", and Father says, "But it was too low to catch jackrabbits, they'd jump over it" and I say; "That's what the mud was for to make 'em slip", and they don't know whether I'm just a moron or the biggest bald-faced liar they've ever seen; so Father he calls me a moron and he beats me, and Mother she calls me a liar and she beats me, and I'm thinking, "Hey, I'm either one or the other so how about making up your minds". *(Pause, drinks)* And that just goes to show you, Meenie, the hardest thing in the world, the loneliest of professions, the job you got to work the hardest at is—having a good time. *(Pause; drinks)*

(REV JOHNSON *and* MRS JOHNSON *wander off*)

RIP: Nice to see her husband taking some time with her. Get her to relax.

SURVEYOR: Still, I said, damn it!!!!

RIP: *(To himself)* Shouldn't yell at a boy. Boys are boys. And they don't stand still. *(Drinks)* Ahhhh. So where's this paper I got to sign?

MEENIE: I gave it to Mother and she sent me out looking for you.

RIP: Seems everybody's always looking for Rip. "Where's Rip?" "Will somebody please go find Rip!" That's why I have so much time, I'm the only one who doesn't waste his days looking for Rip. Don't they know a man's gotta have time to himself?!

(Drinks; MEENIE turns away.)

RIP: I don't mean you child. I'm always glad to see you. Let me look at my girl. Stand up.

(MEENIE does.)

RIP: No, I don't think I deserve to have a thing like you.

MEENIE: I thought you hurt your head.

RIP: Oh, it's hurting all right, Meenie.

MEENIE: I thought a horse kicked you.

RIP: A horse? I get kicked by a lot of horses. There's one in there now, kicking the bejesus out of me.... No, you're too good for a drunk. Heinrich—boy, don't you ever drink.

HEINRICH: *(Trying to stand perfectly still)* Yes, Rip.

RIP: *(To MEENIE)* Give me that cup. Shouldn't drink from a bottle in front of children. *(Pours and drinks)* Did I ever tell you about how my Grandfather got all this land?

MEENIE: No.

RIP: *(Laughs)* I'm sure I have. You're a smart girl, Meenie. Only a girl and already she knows about men. You'll make a good wife.

HEINRICH: *(Still)* I know.

RIP: You do, do you?

MEENIE: I'll make a good wife for Heinrich.

RIP: For Heinrich? So it's settled, is it?

HEINRICH: *(Still)* We've worked it all out, Rip. *(Yells)* I'm standing still!!!!!

MEENIE: He's going to go with his Uncle in a ship to the North Pole, to catch whales.

RIP: The North Pole? That's a long way from here.

HEINRICH: My Uncle will pay me ten shillings a month and I'll send it all to Meenie.

RIP: He's going to send it all to you, Meenie.

MEENIE: And I'll give it all to you to keep for us.

RIP: I wouldn't do that, darling. No. Don't do that. *(Drinks)*

SURVEYOR: Come on, what's going on over there?!!

MEENIE: Shut up!!!!!

RIP: *(Holds his head.)* I thought I heard Gretchen there for a second. *(Drinks)* Heinrich?

HEINRICH: Yes, sir.

RIP: If you marry my daughter, you must promise me something. You must promise me, never to drink.

HEINRICH: I already told you I won't, Rip.

RIP: That's a good boy. Then let's swear on that. The two of us. Not another drop—once I've finished this. *(Drinks)* I was going to tell you how Grandfather got his land. *(Drinks)* He got it by falling off a coach. And that's the God's honest truth. He was going north in the coach and he was drinking and he falls off and it's a hot day, so he takes off his clothes while he's trying to find his way. A coat there. His shoes over here. Well, after he'd made a few miles, he only has his drawers left, so he sits down and as he always slept in his drawers anyway, he's comfortable and he falls asleep. And that's how he got his land.

HEINRICH: Because he fell asleep?

RIP: Because, don't you see, all his clothes that he'd scattered around, they are like claims and as this land hadn't been claimed by nobody yet but some Indians, when he wakes up he finds he'd claimed half a county. He did. *(Drinks)* And that's what my Grandpa told me, little Rip, while I was on his knee. He says: my boy, some men they work all their lives and get nothin', and some men they get drunk and wake up owning half a county. You never know, he says. That's just life, he says. *(Drinks)* Now there's no more land to wake up to. *(Pause)* The time of the lazy fellas like me is over. *(Pause. Stands up, finishes bottle.)* Let's go see if your future father-in-law will give me a drink, Meenie.

HEINRICH: Rip, I thought you were quitting.

RIP: Don't be a smart ass. Give me that. *(Takes the plumb-bob)*

SURVEYOR: Hey!!!!!!

(RIP's hands shake.)

HEINRICH: Why are your hands shaking?

RIP: I said, don't be a smart ass.

(RIP throws down the plumb-bob; RIP, MEENIE, and HEINRICH leave.)

SURVEYOR: *(Throws down his map)* Discipline. No discipline.

SOLDIER: *(Entering with satchels)* What's the matter with you?

SURVEYOR: Those the supplies?

SOLDIER: Yes.

SURVEYOR: Let's go to the next village.

SOLDIER: Why the sudden rush?

PART ONE 33

SURVEYOR: *(Picking up map)* Problem with maps is they keep changing. *(He leaves.)*

SOLDIER: *(Picking up the equipment)* The problem with maps???? *(Leaving)* The problem with you is that you can't stand still!!

(They're gone. Pause. REV JOHNSON *and* MRS JOHNSON *enter. He holds her hand.)*

REV JOHNSON: They're gone. Come on, I know a shed just over the hill.

MRS JOHNSON: Not now. Please.

REV JOHNSON: Pick up the bed spread.

MRS JOHNSON: *(She does.)* No. I don't want to. Please.

REV JOHNSON: I'll carry something if you wish.

*(*MRS JOHNSON *cries.)*

REV JOHNSON: Come. *(He starts to undo her blouse.)* We won't be seen. *(He unbuttons his shirt.)* Do you want me to keep my collar on?

*(*MRS JOHNSON *cries.)*

REV JOHNSON: All you have to do is lie still. Just stay still… And relax.

*(*MRS JOHNSON *and* REV JOHNSON *leave; she cries. Wind)*

Scene Six

(Beer Garden. On one pillar there is now a recruitment poster.)

*(*RIP *at a table. Bottles in front of him. He holds the paper and stares at it, tries to focus on it.* NICK *leans over him;* DERRICK *sits at a distance concentrating on* RIP; COCKLES *stands, anxiously watching* RIP.*)*

(Long pause)

(Suddenly RIP *passes out.)*

(Everyone sighs, shakes their heads, and looks at each other.)

*(*NICK *picks up a bucket of water and pours it over* RIP's *head.)*

RIP: Ahhhhhh! *(Holds his head)* I don't feel so good. What's this? More liquor? When it rains is pours. I haven't seen so much liquor since a wake.

DERRICK: That's what this is, we're paying our last respects to the old Rip.

RIP: The old Rip? Oh right. I forgot. This is Rip's last meal. Once I sign this paper, I become a new man…. *(Holds his head.)* Sit down with me, Nick. I don't like it with everybody watchin' me. Here, let's the both of us drink, like we always do…. Except this'll be the last time, Nick. No more after this.

NICK: If you keeeeep your oath.

RIP: I will. This time I will. I never signed an oath before. Always just said it. Big difference. This here. I'll keep it alright. It's the signing that makes the big. *(Starts to nod off)*

NICK: Then for old times, Rip. *(Sits)*

RIP: Huh? Good. That a boy, Nick. For old…for the old…Rip. Poor old Rip. He weren't so terrible, you know. We were friends, Rip and me. Brothers! …And I don't want to hear nobody say a word against… If I hear so much as a…they'll be sorry. Here's to Rip! My very best friend! *(Drinks. Pause; suddenly)* Who's got a pen!

*(*COCKLES *hurries to give him one;* RIP *feels the pen to see if it's right.)*

RIP: This the pen? Yes. *(Pause)* Somebody read me this again. I want to hear it again.

DERRICK: Cockles.

PART ONE

COCKLES: *("Reading")* "Know all men by these presents, that I, Rip Van Winkle, in consideration for...the monthly salary of sixteen shillings to be paid by Derrick Works, do promise from this time forward to suspend all consumption of liquor, wines, and spirits and thereby to announce to the world that I am a new man." *(Sets the paper back down)*

RIP: There it is again— "new man". I like that— "new man".

*(*RIP *passes out.* NICK *leaves.* GRETCHEN *enters.)*

GRETCHEN: *(To* DERRICK*)* He sign yet? *(He shakes his head.)* You think it's a good idea to get him drunk? If I know Rip, he'll say he wasn't in his right mind, so the oath won't count.

DERRICK: By tomorrow, with my foreman keeping him busy, you keeping an eye on him, Nick locking him out, and with every cent he earns going directly to you, I think there's a chance.

GRETCHEN: I pray you're right. *(Long pause)* Why doesn't he just sign it?!

DERRICK: He will.

GRETCHEN: Why are you doing this?

DERRICK: *(After a pause)* I...

*(*NICK *has entered with bucket. He pours it over* RIP's *head, who wakes up. He doesn't see* GRETCHEN.*)*

RIP: This fine schnapps.

NICK: High Dutch Schchchnapps. Fifteen years in the bottttttle.

RIP: No.

NICK: Last time I touched that schnapps was your wedding. RRRRRRRip. Remember, we broached the keg under that tree.

RIP: This the same?

NICK: Yes.

RIP: I thought I knew my liquor. You had it fifteen years? I wouldn't have had it so long…that was more than fifteen years ago.

NICK: No.

RIP: Same day as I got married.

NICK: Yes.

RIP: Right. Right. The same day. Now don't argue with me, because I'll remember that day as long as I live.

DERRICK: *(Feet up, looks at* GRETCHEN*)* And I remember Gretchen then. I envied you, Rip.

(GRETCHEN *looks at him.*)

RIP: No! Yes? I guess I envied me too. *(Drinks)* You didn't know what was happening, did you Derrick?

DERRICK: *(Watching* GRETCHEN*)* She was lovely.

RIP: Who?

DERRICK: Your wife.

RIP: Gretchen lovely??? I guess she was. Yeh, she was my little girl then. We were handsome together.

DERRICK: To me, Rip, she was like some wonderful thing that was just out of my reach.

RIP: *(Sighs)* Too bad I've not been out of her reach. *(Rubs his face)* Nick, have another.

(NICK *begins to pour water in his drink.*)

RIP: Hey, stop that! I thought you were a drinking man. Don't you know good liquor and water is like a man and his wife?

NICK: How soooo?

PART ONE

RIP: They never agree! *(Laughs)* I always take my liquor single. Here's to your good health! May you live long and happy!

DERRICK: And prosper.

RIP: Yeh.

(They drink. GRETCHEN, *still unseen by* RIP, *watches. Pause)*

DERRICK: That's right, Rip; drink away and drown your sorrows.

RIP: Yes, but she won't drown.

(Everyone turns to GRETCHEN, *except* RIP, *who drinks.)*

RIP: My wife is my sorrow and you can't drown her. She came close once, but couldn't do it.

NICK: When? *(Turns to* GRETCHEN*)*

RIP: Didn't you know that Gretchen almost drowned?

NICK: No.

RIP: That was the funniest thing. It was the same day we got married; she was coming across the river in the ferryboat and…

DERRICK: And what, Rip?

RIP: And the boat, it turned over.

DERRICK: Turned over?

RIP: Yes. But too bad she wasn't on it.

(Pause. GRETCHEN, *obviously hurt, just watches.)*

DERRICK: *(More to* GRETCHEN *than* RIP*)* Why too bad, Rip?

RIP: You got to ask? Because she… *(Drinks)*

DERRICK: Because?

RIP: See that's what I was sayin', Nick, if she had been in that boat like she was supposed to be, she'd have drowned. I don't know how she got left behind. Women are always late—always. *(Drinks)* Course if she were drowning I would have jumped in to save her....

(GRETCHEN *sort of smiles.*)

RIP: At least I think I'd have done that. Yes, I would have done that, because then it would have been more my duty than it would be today. If she was drowning today I don't know what I'd do.... *(Laughs)*

(GRETCHEN *starts to go to* RIP; DERRICK *motions for her to stop.*)

DERRICK: You wouldn't save Gretchen?

RIP: *(Drinks)* It's only when I'm drunk that I tell her what I think, and then she don't listen 'cause she says I'm drunk. *(Drinks)* I pity her.

DERRICK: You pity Gretchen?

RIP: Yeh. Why else would I keep her around unless I pitied her? I got a big heart, that's why I don't kick her out. Stupid woman.

(Pause)

DERRICK: *(To* GRETCHEN*)* Gretchen?

(GRETCHEN *shakes her head.*)

RIP: Who else I been talking about? Of course, Gretchen. Stupid and ugly and dumb as a brick. *(Laughs)* Maybe I should just throw her out. Yah, maybe that's what I'll do. *(Laughs)*

(NICK, *getting nervous, stands and starts to back away.*)

RIP: Hey, where you going? There's still your drink.

NICK: I I I I I...

RIP: I'm talking! I need to have my friends.

NICK: *(Looking at* GRETCHEN.*)* Riiiiiip...

RIP: You think I'm boasting, don't you? Well you just wait and see what I do to that bitch of mine, you'll see that I'm not... *(Sees* GRETCHEN. *Pause)* Gretchen. *(Pause; looks at everyone's face. Breaks down and sobs)* Gretchen!

GRETCHEN: Sign, Rip.

RIP: I hate drinking. I don't want to drink. *(Sobs)* I didn't mean....

GRETCHEN: The liquor was talking.

RIP: I *(Screams)* Yes!!!!!!!!!! *(Pause, calms himself)* That liquor's got a big mouth. *(Looks at* GRETCHEN, *then back to the paper)* Does it take all that pen and ink to say just what Cockles said?

DERRICK: Yes, Rip.

GRETCHEN: Please, Rip.

RIP: And where does my X go, Derrick?

DERRICK: *(Stands, goes to* RIP.*)* There, you see that white space?

RIP: I see it. *(He practices Xs in the air.)*

COCKLES: Sign.

DERRICK: *(To* COCKLES*)* Easy... It's a new life, Rip.

(RIP *looks to* GRETCHEN.)

GRETCHEN: *(Nods)* Rip. *(Looks to* NICK*)*

NICK: Think of Meenie.

(Pause)

RIP: Why do you bother? *(Pause)* I'll sign. *(Pause)* But not like this. I'm not going to let the new Rip be born drunk...and looking like.... No. I want some clean clothes. And water so I can wash. And something like coffee to get me sober. And then we're all going to see a new Rip who doesn't look a thing like me. *(Looks up)* It's the least we can do for the new Rip, isn't it?

(Pause)

GRETCHEN: *(Finally)* I'll fetch his clothes. *(To* DERRICK*)* Keep an eye on him.

(GRETCHEN *leaves. Pause)*

DERRICK: *(Throws down the butt of his cigar; to* COCKLES*)* I'm getting some more cigars. Watch him.

(DERRICK *leaves. Pause.* RIP *takes a glass and pours it over his head to sober up.)*

COCKLES: Look after him, will you? I've got to get rid of this beer.

(Pause. HEINRICH *enters.)*

NICK: Don't let him leave. *(He leaves.)*

RIP: Tell me, do you ever cry, boy?

HEINRICH: Never.

RIP: *(Nods)* That's because you don't drink.

(HEINRICH *turns away.)*

RIP: Don't go away. So you're going to marry my daughter.

HEINRICH: Yes, sir. *(Turns again)*

RIP: I said talk to me. Stay here. *(Not really looking at* HEINRICH*)* Tell me about yourself. Do you go to school?

HEINRICH: Sometimes, when my father can spare me.

RIP: *(Not really listening.)* Ah. So you go to school?

HEINRICH: Yes.

RIP: And. And what do you learn in school? Important things?

HEINRICH: Yes; reading, writing, and arithmetic.

RIP: All that? I don't see how the little mind can stand it all. Can you read?

PART ONE

HEINRICH: I just told you I could.

RIP: I forgot. You aren't lying to me are you, 'cause if you can't read, I won't let you marry my daughter. I won't have anybody in my family who can't read. Except me. And Gretchen.

HEINRICH: I can prove to you I can read—I'll read you that poster.

RIP: You do that, boy. Read it to me.

HEINRICH: "All able bodied men bear arms. And fight for freedom against the tyranny of the King."

RIP: It says that?

HEINRICH: Yes.

RIP: The King, huh? I've never seen any King around here.... How do I know you're not making all that up? Here. You read this, because I already know what it says. *(Hands him the paper)*

HEINRICH: "Know all men by these presents..."

RIP: Yeh. That's right. What a wonderful thing reading is—why you read it pretty near as well as Cockles. Go on.

HEINRICH: "That I, Rip Van Winkle..."

RIP: That's my name. You'll be a good son-in-law. Go on.

HEINRICH: "...in consideration for sums received do hereby sell and convey to Mister Hans Derrick all my estate, houses, lands whatsoever—"

RIP: What are you reading?! That's not down there!

HEINRICH: See— "houses", "lands", "whatsoever". *(Pause)*

RIP: Are you lying to me, son? *(Stares at him.)* Go on with the rest.

HEINRICH: "Whereof he now holds possession by mortgaged deeds, from time to time executed by me." That's all there is.

(Pause; RIP shakes his head.)

RIP: You read it better than Cockles, my boy. Much better. *(Puts paper in his pocket; without looking up)* Now run along and leave me by myself.

(HEINRICH leaves; RIP slaps his head.)

RIP: Like a brick. *(He stands. Silence)* Whore.

(RIP starts to leave, stops, goes back and takes a bottle and leaves. Short pause. GRETCHEN *enters with clothes;* DERRICK *enters with cigars;* COCKLES *enters buttoning up his pants, and* NICK *enters to clear off more bottles—all at the same time, all from different directions. They stop.)*

DERRICK: Where'd he go?

NICK: He's gone.

GRETCHEN: He's gone.

COCKLES: He's gone.

(Short pause)

GRETCHEN: I'll kill him.

(Short pause)

COCKLES: *(To* DERRICK; *hopeful)* Maybe she will.

(Crash of thunder)

Scene Seven

(RIP's cottage. Night Storm rages. MEENIE *at the window. Pause.* GRETCHEN *enters, wet.)*

GRETCHEN: Where's your father?

MEENIE: He's not come home.

GRETCHEN: Coward. He's got the courage of a mouse. Let him just try to walk in like nothing's happened. I'd like to see that. If he's got a brain, he won't.

MEENIE: He's got a brain.

GRETCHEN: Meenie, don't talk to me now.

MEENIE: Mother, don't be so hard.

GRETCHEN: Me?!! Is that how you see this? I'm being too hard? Meenie, don't make me hit you...I'm not the one who's thrown away two good jobs in one day! ... Now what are you crying for?

MEENIE: Because my father's out in the rain.

(Thunder—MEENIE screams.)

GRETCHEN: He gets what he deserves. Do him good to get soaked from the outside for a change. *(Pause)* Is supper ready?

MEENIE: It's there by the fireside. Shall I lay the table?

GRETCHEN: Yes. *(Thunder)* What an awful night. I'm exhausted. *(She sits.)* Who's there? *(To herself)* The wind.

MEENIE: Shall I lay the table for two or for three?

GRETCHEN: Two! He won't get supper here tonight. Let him eat the mud.

(Thunder)

GRETCHEN: Just like him to go running around in this weather. I'll have him sick and on my hands for a week. And that will be his excuse to do nothing. *(Short pause; listens—nothing)* Where is he?!... This time I am putting my foot down—going to put it down hard on his head. *(Fighting back tears)* If he only knew how he hurts me.

(Thunder)

GRETCHEN: I don't know why I bother to even worry; I could be on my death bed, and he'd still expect me to wait on him.

(Lightning)

GRETCHEN: That was quite a flash. He's out there drunk and when he's drunk he doesn't know the first thing about taking care of himself… Oh Meenie, the gall he had to say he pitied me. And that little boy face—how he looked when he saw me, I…I fell for it. Again. Again I fell for it. *(Stands)* Go ahead and kill yourself!!!!

(Knock at the door; pause)

MEENIE: There he is now!

(MEENIE *opens the door;* HEINRICH *enters.*)

GRETCHEN: Where's Rip? He's not with you?

HEINRICH: I thought he'd be here.

GRETCHEN: He's passed out in the hills, that's where that drunk is. Dogs come in from the rain. Not your father.

HEINRICH: Should I run out and look for him? I know the paths; we've often climbed together.

GRETCHEN: No. I'll bring him back myself. *(Puts on her coat)*

MEENIE: But Mother—if he hears your voice, he'll only run away that much faster.

GRETCHEN: *(Hurt)* Don't Meenie.

MEENIE: But it's true!

GRETCHEN: Then I can't help that. Let him run. Least then the neighbors will know I tried and won't go blaming me.

(GRETCHEN *leaves. Pause*)

HEINRICH: I hope your father hasn't gone to the mountains tonight, Meenie.

MEENIE: He'll die from the cold, I know it!

HEINRICH: *(Seriously)* It's not that. I've just heard old Clausen over at father's saying that on this night every fifteen years, the ghosts—

MEENIE: *(Catching his wrist)* The what?

HEINRICH: The ghosts of Hendrick Hudson and his pirate crew visit the Catskills.

MEENIE: Ghosts?! Father!!!!

HEINRICH: Sh-sh! And the spirits have been seen there smoking, drinking, and playing tenpins.

MEENIE: Tenpins? *(Short pause; as she thinks.)* Don't be silly. I don't believe it.

HEINRICH: And every time that Hendrick Hudson lights his pipe, there is a flash of lightning.

(Lightning; MEENIE *gasps. Pause)*

HEINRICH: And when he rolls the balls along...

(Rolling thunder)

HEINRICH: ...there is a peal of thunder.

*(*HEINRICH *and* MEENIE *both listen, then crash of thunder;* MEENIE *screams. Door bangs open.* RIP *enters helping in* MRS JOHNSON, *whose face is bruised.)*

MEENIE: Father!

HEINRICH: Rip!

RIP: I found Mrs Johnson out in the hills. She's hurt. Get her dry.

MRS JOHNSON: I'm not hurt bad. Don't go to any trouble. I can take care of myself.

HEINRICH: What was she doing out there in this storm?

RIP: Get something hot, Meenie. There, sit by the fire. Where's your Mother—over at Derrick's would be my guess.

MEENIE: She went out looking for you.

RIP: Ah, I'm sure she did. Looking to finish off what she wounded. *(Takes out the paper, pats it, puts it back)* Well, let her try.

HEINRICH: Heinrich, look at her face! What did you do—fall down?

MRS JOHNSON: Yes. Yes. I fell.

MEENIE: Father, where have you been?

RIP: *(Looks at her)* Washing my wound.

(GRETCHEN *enters, stops, stares at* RIP *then suddenly sees* MRS JOHNSON.)

GRETCHEN: Mrs Johnson!

MEENIE: Her face, Mother.

GRETCHEN: *(Quickly)* She's soaked. Meenie, hurry and get my Sunday dress. *(To* RIP*)* You, I'll talk to later—when we don't have company.

RIP: I'll talk to you now, you whore.

GRETCHEN: What? What?

RIP: *(Slaps her)* Whore! Whore!

(She screams.)

MEENIE: Father!

GRETCHEN: You drunk!!!!! *(She pulls away from him, turns to* MEENIE*)* Take Mrs Johnson into the other room. And please close the door.

(MEENIE *and* MRS JOHNSON *leave.*)

RIP: *(Looking at his hand)* Like a rabid dog, that's what you scratch like.

GRETCHEN: Why Rip? *(Suddenly erupts, grabs a chair and throws it at him)* Why?!!!!!!!!

RIP: *(Very frustrated)* That's my question!!! Why? Why does my wife want to keep me begging and crawling? Who else knew? Nick? Mecnic? I hurt so much.

GRETCHEN: Suffer.

RIP: You hate me?

GRETCHEN: *(After a short pause)* Yes.

RIP: You hate me?

GRETCHEN: Yes.

RIP: *(Nods)* She admits it. You and Derrick were pretty smart. Jesus Christ, she admits it to my face!!!! Give me a cane, 'cause I'm a blind man. Keep me drunk so I don't see what's in front of my own nose.

(RIP reaches for a bottle, GRETCHEN grabs it away.)

GRETCHEN: Mine. Because it's in my house.

RIP: The bottle.

GRETCHEN: Empty.

RIP: No.

GRETCHEN: Will be. *(She opens it)*

RIP: The bottle or I break apart the house.

GRETCHEN: No, Rip.

RIP: Will.

GRETCHEN: Here. *(She starts to pour some on the floor.)*

RIP: Stop, or I don't stop me. *(Picks up a plate)*

GRETCHEN: You wouldn't.

RIP: Done it two or three times before, haven't I?

(GRETCHEN hesitates then pours some more on the floor. RIP smashes a plate.)

GRETCHEN: Stop him!!!!!

MEENIE: *(Who has returned)* Father!

RIP: Maybe I'm your father and maybe I'm not.

(MEENIE cries.)

GRETCHEN: Rip how can you?!!!!

RIP: *(With more plates)* Sign—you said. Sign. Well here's my X! *(Smashes more plates)*

HEINRICH: I'll get my father. *(Runs out)*

GRETCHEN: All for a bottle. Of course. That's appropriate. That always has come first.

RIP: What else do I have?

(Long pause)

GRETCHEN: Nothing.

MEENIE: Father, what are you doing?

RIP: Packing.

GRETCHEN: You're not walking out on me, because I'm throwing you out.

RIP: I was thrown out years ago. But this is the first time I'm walking out… Why don't you cry—maybe clean your soul.

GRETCHEN: Out! Out! You disgrace this house!!

RIP: Yes. If not being a sinner in a house of sin is a disgrace, then that's just what I am. *(Starts to leave with his gun. Stops)* If I weren't drunk, I'd do the Lord a favor and butcher you myself.

GRETCHEN: Try it! Try it!

(RIP leaves; slams the door)

MEENIE: Father!!! Father!!!

(GRETCHEN sits. Pause. Knock on the door. They look up. Door opens. REV JOHNSON appears. Long pause)

GRETCHEN: *(Quietly)* She's in there. *(Points to the other room)*

(REV JOHNSON *goes into the other room. We hear him beating his wife. She screams and sobs.*)

Scene Eight

(A path in the mountains. The storm. Night. RIP *enters with his head down, coat-collar up. He protects his gun with the skin of his jacket.)*

RIP: *(To himself)* Cold. Cold and wet... Except inside. In there it's hot like an oven. Strange...I better look for someplace, maybe a cave, that's dry. Looks like this'll go on all night... *(Looks around)* Funny how everything sort of reminds me of her. The way the wind howls—that's how she talks to me. The way the ground feels—those are her kisses. But better. The ground's better. *(Starts to go)* Hey, what happened to my dog? He was with me just a moment ago. Something must have scared him. The thunder. *(Nods)* Too bad—I could have used the company. Wet. *(Lightning)* What a flash that was. Old Hendrick Hudson's lighting his pipe tonight. *(Laughs)* Now we'll hear him roll his big bowling balls along. *(Listens—thunder)* There it is. *(Looks to his left)* Is that my dog? No. Whatever it is it's got two legs, not four. Looks like a boy. Does. Didn't think I'd see anyone up this high, least not on a night like tonight. Hey! Over here! You! *(Moves to his left)* He's gone. Where'd he go? That's funny. I would have sworn I saw somebody over there. Must have been a shadow. *(Looks to his right)* There's another one. Hey, you! Mister! Don't run away! I don't want to hurt you!

*(*RIP *runs off right. A strange dwarfish* FIGURE *enters left. He has a long beard, carries a keg on his shoulders.* RIP *returns, backing in, doesn't notice the* FIGURE.*)*

RIP: Strange. He was there a second ago. Boy, my eyes must be playin' tricks. I better find me a place soon or God knows what I'm going to start seeing. *(Bumps into the* FIGURE. *Screams)* Ahhhhhh! You scared me. Jesus. Where'd you come from? I didn't see you. *(Pause. No response)* Were those your pals I was seeing? What are you doing up here? You got a cabin somewhere?... Talkative aren't you... But a good listener, I'll bet.

(FIGURE *sets down the keg.*)

RIP: What's that in the keg? Not liquor, is it? I ain't had any liquor myself for...well, not since I finished my bottle, and that was a good half hour ago.

(FIGURE *tries to light his pipe—lightning.*)

RIP: Feels like it's getting closer. Where you going with that? Far?

(No response. Thunder)

RIP: That's old Hendrick Hudson and his bowling balls.

(Laughs, FIGURE *stares at him;* RIP's *laugh peters out.)*

RIP: Tell me something, are your women folk as quiet as you? If they are I'd really like to meet 'em. I'd never believe that a woman could keep her mouth shut unless I saw it with my own eyes. *(Laughs, no response)* You know you're an awfully small fellow to carry such a big keg. You need some help? You see, that's how we are around here—helpful. We help each other out; watch each other's kids; look after each other when we're sick; buy each other drinks.

(FIGURE *tries to light his pipe again—lightning.*)

RIP: Whoa. See what I mean? Feel how close it's getting?

(FIGURE *tries again—lightning.*)

PART ONE

RIP: Having trouble lighting that thing? Here, let me help you. I know how hard it is when it's windy. *(He tries to light the* FIGURE's *pipe—each try—lightning. Finally succeeds)* There you go.

(FIGURE *picks up the keg and starts to go.*)

RIP: How far's the cabin?

(FIGURE *turns back and looks at him.*)

RIP: Don't worry, I'm right behind you…. You know, it's a good thing you came along, I was beginning to wonder whether I was going to get any sleep tonight.

(FIGURE *and* RIP *exit. Roll of thunder*)

END OF PART ONE

PART TWO
"HUNGOVER"

Scene One

(The mountains. Fifteen years later. Dawn. RIP *lies on the ground, his hair and beard are long and white, his clothes are rags, his hands old and weather beaten, and when he speaks, his voice is hoarse and feeble. Long pause.* RIP *starts to wake up. He groans, in obvious pain.)*

RIP: Hurt. Hurt. The neck. Feels like someone's got their hands around my neck. Ow! ...What's the problem with my elbow? *(Tries to rub it, screams in pain)* Ahhhhhhh!!!!!... The other one hurts even more.... Bright sun. All I see are spots. *(Pause)* Where the hell am I? Did I sleep out here all night? No wonder it hurts to move. You get rheumatism sleeping in the wet grass. And that's just what I got. *(Coughs, then chokes)* Throat's like a bone. *(Tries to get up, grimaces)* Never had rheumatism like this. *(Suddenly cries out)* Pain!!!... My body's pretty angry with me. *(Suddenly remembers)* Wait a minute.... Nah, I must have dreamed it. Though those queer fellas seemed real enough. And strange things do happen.... *(Laughs to himself)* especially when you're drunk. *(He rises—reaches for his gun, which falls apart.)* My gun's got rheumatism too.... Someone must have took my good gun and left me this thing.... Maybe them?... Nah, that was a dream, Rip. *(Looks out over the valley)* What's that? That's not my village. That's more than twice the size of my village. But it sort of looks like my village, but bigger.... Maybe I'm still dreaming. Maybe. *(Shakes his head)* I don't know. *(Starts to go slowly)* My backbone is broke. *(Moves a few more steps)* My head's full of rocks. *(Few more steps)* This is the worst hangover I ever had. *(Falls; slowly gets up)* I don't know. *(He leaves.)*

(Pause)

(HENRY *enters. He is a Canuck.)*

HENRY: Ho! Ho!

(FRANCIS *and* JACK, *two Canucks, run in.)*

FRANCIS: Sh-sh. Light.

HENRY: *(Nods, whispers)* I've seen him.

FRANCIS: Who?

HENRY: Him!

FRANCIS: Yes? Yes?

HENRY: He's going to bring more money.

FRANCIS: He's with us then.

HENRY: Yes.

JACK: Wooed and won.

HENRY: Yes.

FRANCIS: And his uncle?

HENRY: He's lost everything.

FRANCIS: His uncle?

HENRY: No, Cockles. He's been cut out. There was a party. He's with us.

FRANCIS: Good. Good. So he brings more money.

HENRY: And he says, we fight. He says the offices are first. We should burn 'em.

PART TWO

FRANCIS: The offices?!

HENRY: That's where the deeds are.

FRANCIS: I know. I know. But who cares about deeds? They'll just make more deeds. They made the deeds they got now, didn't they? We want the land back. Not deeds.

HENRY: He says, first the offices, because that'll confuse 'em.

FRANCIS: Fuck the offices.

HENRY: Because that'll confuse them! Then the works.

JACK: The works?

FRANCIS: Oh.

HENRY: Yes.

FRANCIS: Burn 'em?

HENRY: Yes.

FRANCIS: That sounds more like it. Burn the works. Good.

JACK: They'll give us back our valley then.

FRANCIS: Give us nothing. We take it.

JACK: And take theirs.

HENRY: Maybe.

JACK: They take ours. We take theirs.

HENRY: What we want with two valleys?

JACK: What they want with two valleys?

FRANCIS: Where's he now?

HENRY: Getting the money.

FRANCIS: Oh.

JACK: You weren't seen?

HEINRICH: There was a party. Everybody drunk. This morning everybody going to hurt.

JACK: Good. Good.

Scene Two

(The garden of DERRICK'*s house. Morning. Chairs. Picket fence. Gate. Path, upstage of the fence. Bottles, dishes, etc. about—the aftermath of a party)*

(Servant GIRL *and* HOUSEKEEPER *are cleaning up.* DERRICK's SECRETARY *sits; he drinks coffee.)*

GIRL: And then?

SECRETARY: *(To* HOUSEKEEPER*)* Big nose on that girl.

(HOUSEKEEPER *nods.)*

GIRL: Can I help it if I was made to stay in the kitchen? So what happened then?!!!

SECRETARY: Mister Derrick—well, you could tell something was on his mind, because he had a little smile that sort of ran across his lips, and relaxed, I hadn't seen him so relaxed in months—so you could tell something was up, but you didn't know what. And he's filling everyone's glass, and then when he's through, he bangs the table....

GIRL: This table?

SECRETARY: I think so.

GIRL: So he was here and Miss Meenie?

SECRETARY: She was—standing there I think.

GIRL: With the schoolteacher.

SECRETARY: No. No. The schoolteacher he leans against the fence. He doesn't talk to anyone. He just smokes a pipe and leans.

PART TWO

HOUSEKEEPER: He doesn't lean.

SECRETARY: He does. He's leaning.

HOUSEKEEPER: He's sitting.

SECRETARY: Leaning. On the gate. It was the gate he was leaning against.

HOUSEKEEPER: And he doesn't smoke a pipe.

GIRL: So Mister Derrick pounds.

SECRETARY: Yes. And everybody stops talking, and so they're looking at him and he says— "allow me to make a personal announcement." And everybody is looking at everybody because nobody has said to anybody anything about any personal announcement.

HOUSEKEEPER: I knew.

SECRETARY: No you didn't. How could you? Nobody knew. I didn't know. Did you?

(HOUSEKEEPER *shrugs and smiles.*)

SECRETARY: *(To* GIRL*)* She didn't know. And so he says—and he has his glass raised—he says: "to my dear step-daughter Meenie, and to her betrothed!"

GIRL: Oh!

SECRETARY: And everyone's craning their necks to look at everyone who's craning their necks.

GIRL: So no one did know.

SECRETARY: No one knew. Not even me.

HOUSEKEEPER: I knew.

SECRETARY: *(Trying to ignore her)* And then the schoolteacher he takes his pipe out of his mouth— he was smoking—and he moves away from the fence—on which he had been leaning—and slowly he approaches Meenie—and the faces on everybody, one small breeze would have knocked us all over—and the schoolteacher, he is taking Meenie's hand, now he's kissing it and Meenie is blushing and Mister Derrick, he shouts: "to the bride and groom!" And everybody applauded! But while they applauded they're looking around to see who knew while at the same time trying to look like they knew.

GIRL: No.

SECRETARY: Yes.

HOUSEKEEPER: No.

SECRETARY: Yes! ...Like bees in a hive, there's buzzing. And the men, they slap the schoolteacher on the back and he looks embarrassed—but happy too; and the women they're saying: "how wonderful" to Meenie and they grab their husbands and say "did you know?" and Seth, the fiddler, plays and Mister Derrick, I didn't know he could play the mouth organ, but he can and does and that's about when everybody starts to dance—first Meenie and the schoolteacher, of course, but then everybody—but only Meenie and the schoolteacher are really dancing, the rest are just sort of moving their feet because they're busy talking, and then Mister Derrick dances with Meenie, and Gretchen with the schoolteacher and she looks like a mother all right—she has tears in her eyes but she can't stop laughing and she steps on the schoolteacher's foot and almost falls down but he holds her up and then everybody dances with Meenie or with the schoolteacher and that's pretty much what happened.

HOUSEKEEPER: No, it isn't. He didn't say "to the bride and groom", Mister Derrick said "prosit" and pointed.

SECRETARY: He said "to the bride and groom."

HOUSEKEEPER: "Prosit" and pointed. I know, because I wasn't drunk.

(Pause)

PART TWO

GIRL: And what about Cockles? I thought Mister Derrick had been so set on Meenie marrying him.

SECRETARY: Must have changed his mind.

HOUSEKEEPER: He wasn't there.

SECRETARY: He was there. He left early.

HOUSEKEEPER: He was invited, but he didn't come.

SECRETARY: They didn't invite him, but he came anyway, but only stayed for a minute or two.

GIRL: It's incredible, isn't it?

HOUSEKEEPER: What is?

SECRETARY: Everything. In a young girl's eyes, everything's incredible.

GIRL: No, that it could have been Cockles, instead of the schoolteacher. Everybody thought it'd be Cockles, nobody thought about the schoolteacher.

HOUSEKEEPER: I had my eye on the schoolteacher.

GIRL: And if she hadn't waited so long for the Vedder boy to come back from the war—

SECRETARY: *(To himself nodding)* Heinrich.

HOUSEKEEPER: I know who the Vedder boy is!

GIRL: If she hadn't waited it would have been Cockles, because nobody thought about the schoolteacher, not even Meenie, because he wasn't even here then.

SECRETARY: No. She's right. Poor Cockles.

HOUSEKEEPER: Nice man.

(Pause)

SECRETARY: Yes. *(Pause)* I wonder if he knew.

GIRL: Sh-sh! Here he comes!

HOUSEKEEPER: Cockles?!!

GIRL: *(Loud whisper)* Yes!!

(COCKLES *comes around the corner—the servants become busy. He carries a small case. He comes through the gate. He is strangely distant.*)

COCKLES: I hear I missed quite the spectacular party.

HOUSEKEEPER: Told you he wasn't here.

SECRETARY: I'm sorry you had to miss it.

COCKLES: Whole town's buzzing with the news. Quite a surprise for everyone. Schoolteacher's a fortunate man. I couldn't be happier. *(To* GIRL*)* Do you believe me?

GIRL: Yes.

COCKLES: *(Shakes his head, laughs; to* SECRETARY*)* Is my Uncle in his study?

SECRETARY: He isn't up yet.

COCKLES: No. Of course not. It was a long evening…. For everyone…I haven't been to sleep myself.

SECRETARY: No?

COCKLES: I could hear the music. I love to dance. *(Awkward pause)* I'll wait in the study. *(Leaves)*

HOUSEKEEPER: Did you see his face?

SECRETARY: Chalk.

GIRL: He said he didn't sleep.

HOUSEKEEPER: Who could? I couldn't.

SECRETARY: *(To* GIRL*)* I forgot to tell you the other news.

GIRL: There's more?!

SECRETARY: Listen. Mister Derrick, well he's been drinking for quite a while now, and he pounds the table again and he begins to wave a piece of paper in the air like it was a banner and he says: "who knows what this is?" And of course nobody knows, though of course nobody says that they don't know, and he says: "it is my will".

GIRL: His will!

SECRETARY: His will. And then he says: "my wedding present" and he hands it first to the schoolteacher who reads it and his mouth it won't close, and then Meenie takes it and then Gretchen and then someone gets it and then finally I get it and I read it and it says...that when Mister Derrick dies, the works, they will belong to Meenie and the schoolteacher. That is what it says.

GIRL: To Meenie and the schoolteacher?

SECRETARY: Yes.

GIRL: But everybody has always said Cockles was going to inherit the works. What with him being Mister Derrick's nephew.

SECRETARY: I know. That's what everybody thought. That's what Cockles thought.

(Pause)

GIRL: Poor man.

HOUSEKEEPER: He didn't know. You could tell.

(DERRICK *enters—hungover.*)

DERRICK: Who didn't know what? Is that coffee?

(HOUSEKEEPER *pours him some.*)

SECRETARY: We were talking about the party, sir.

DERRICK: I'm sure you're not the only ones. *(Smiles, flinches in pain, rubs his head)* The head. *(Sits)* The art of surprise is indeed an art. I proved it last night. Our neighbors think they know everything there is to know about the Derricks. But who knew? *(Smiles)*

SECRETARY: *(Points to* HOUSEKEEPER*)* She knew.

DERRICK: *(Surprised)* She did?

HOUSEKEEPER: Not really, sir.

SECRETARY: But she did. She knew everything, Mister Derrick. She told me so.

DERRICK: Then she must have had one eye on the housekeeping and one eye in the key hole.

HOUSEKEEPER: I didn't know. What do I know? Nothing. Nothing.

(HOUSEKEEPER *hurries out;* DERRICK *and* SECRETARY *smile.*)

GIRL: *(As she's leaving, stops before* DERRICK*)* I hear it was a very lovely party, Mister Derrick.

DERRICK: It got the job done.

(GIRL *leaves.*)

DERRICK: *(Referring to the* GIRL*)* Good worker?

SECRETARY: Talkative. *(Points to his nose)* Big nose.

DERRICK: Unlike us. Who mind our own business. *(Sips his coffee.)* I wonder if I shouldn't have been an actor. Obviously, I have the flair for the dramatic. I could have let our news slip out to one of those gossips, but I couldn't resist seeing those faces last night. I don't know why that gave me such a thrill, but it does.

(Pause)

SECRETARY: Cockles is in the study.

DERRICK: That, unfortunately, is no surprise. I'll finish my coffee.

(GRETCHEN *enters—hungover.*)

GRETCHEN: Does it have to be so bright?!

DERRICK: I'll have someone close the curtains.

GRETCHEN: Don't make me laugh. My head jiggles enough just walking. Is that coffee?... *(Takes a cup)* Well, you saw the farmer's daughter in me last night.

Two drinks and the literate elegant wife of the town's leading businessman went to bed. And the farmer's daughter rose from her grave. *(Sits, suddenly has a pain)* With a vengeance.

DERRICK: My memory's a bit blurred.

GRETCHEN: *(To* SECRETARY*)* Would you tell Maria, I'll skip breakfast this morning.

(SECRETARY *leaves.*)

DERRICK: Were you sick?

GRETCHEN: Did you hear?

DERRICK: No.

GRETCHEN: Let's say I gave up what I took.... Since when did you play the mouth organ?

DERRICK: Since when did you sing at parties?

GRETCHEN: Did I sing?

DERRICK: Did I play the mouth organ?

GRETCHEN: *(She laughs, then groans.)* Do you feel as awful as I do?

DERRICK: Worse...Cockles is here. In the study. I haven't seen him yet.

(Pause)

GRETCHEN: Will he give it all back?

DERRICK: It's not the money that I care about. I just want him out of my sight. *(Pause; he stands.)* I'll get this over with.

GRETCHEN: Hans? Do you know where he'll go?

DERRICK: Where do crooks go? Your guess is as good as mine. *(Stands to leave. Stops)* He's my nephew. I raised him. It makes you sick.

(DERRICK *leaves.* GRETCHEN *sighs, pats her head;* MEENIE *appears; she is upset, she has been crying.)*

MEENIE: I'm ashamed.

GRETCHEN: Meenie! Have you been crying? What happened?

MEENIE: You happened! *(She goes to* GRETCHEN *and slaps her across the face.)*

(GRETCHEN *screams and collapses.*)

GRETCHEN: What did I do? What did I do?!

MEENIE: I haven't slept thinking about it. What are you?! You don't know anything!

GRETCHEN: *(Desperate)* Meenie, I don't understand!

MEENIE: Of course he didn't say anything. But I knew what he was thinking. And I wouldn't blame him a bit if he broke off the engagement. I wouldn't want to marry me either.

GRETCHEN: Why, Meenie?????

MEENIE: With a mother like you… How could you get so drunk?!!!!!

GRETCHEN: I got…???? Did I say something awful, Meenie? Did I!!!!!!

MEENIE: He's probably never seen a woman drunk before. He probably didn't know there were women who got drunk. How ashamed I am of you!

GRETCHEN: But it was because I was happy, Meenie.

MEENIE: You were sick. I heard you. I'm thinking—there's my mother and she's on her knees and drunk and retching. Every time you retch I want to scream. Why did you get sick???!!

GRETCHEN: That was after everyone was gone, Meenie.

MEENIE: I wasn't gone!

GRETCHEN: You're being unfair to me, Meenie.

PART TWO

MEENIE: You're a hick! You're a small town hick and you don't even know how to behave!!... He knew. He didn't say anything, but he knew. *(She runs out.)*

(SECRETARY, who has entered and heard most of this approaches GRETCHEN, who is crying. Long pause.)

SECRETARY: If she were mine, I'd whip her 'til she screamed.

GRETCHEN: No.

(COCKLES enters from the house.)

COCKLES: *(As he passes them)* Happy? He didn't fire me....I quit. *(Starts to walk away, turns)* My life's in those works. *(Opens the gate; yells)* I'll bet everybody's happy now!!!!!! *(Slams gate, hurries off. Pause)*

(DERRICK and MEENIE enter.)

DERRICK: *(Entering)* Meenie, I can't understand a word. Can't this wait.

MEENIE: Talk to him. I think he likes you.

DERRICK: Talk to who? Can't it wait?

GRETCHEN: Hans, I don't her.

DERRICK: Blame her for what?

MEENIE: For what?!!!!

SECRETARY: Cockles quit?

MEENIE: Cockles???????

DERRICK: *(To MEENIE)* You want me to talk to Cockles???? But I just talked to him.

MEENIE: No, to James!

DERRICK: James????

MEENIE: Explain to him. Apologize to him.

DERRICK: James?????

SECRETARY: The schoolteacher.

DERRICK: I know who James is!

SECRETARY: Why did he quit?

GRETCHEN: Hans, I told you. I warned you.

DERRICK: About Cockles???

GRETCHEN: About me!! I'm just a farmer's wife!

DERRICK: What?! What?! Quiet!!!

GIRL: *(As she enters with breakfast)* Your breakfast. Mrs Derrick.

GRETCHEN: I said I didn't want breakfast!

MEENIE: Because she'd get sick!!

SECRETARY: It's for Mister Derrick.

DERRICK: I'm not hungry. I'm not hungry! Set it down. *(Screams)* Set it down!!!!!!

(Pause. Everyone is quiet.)

DERRICK: We'll get to this. Whatever it is. We will get to it. But first, Otto, get me the books from the safe…

(SECRETARY *leaves.*)

DERRICK: I'm going to rub his nose in this. How he has the gall to deny, to my face…

GRETCHEN: Who?

DERRICK: Cockles!!!! …It's not stealing, he says. It's a loan. A loan to Canucks!

MEENIE: Canucks????

DERRICK: I ask him, politely, very, very politely: a loan for what? So they can buy guns and shoot me in the back??! So they can farm, he says. So they can pay rent, he says. It's a good business, then why'd he have to fiddle with the books!!!! Otto!!! I didn't fight a war for Canucks! If they wanted to keep their land they should have thought about that when they picked sides. They supported the British, so let the British support them now! Otto!!

(HOUSEKEEPER *runs on.*)

HOUSEKEEPER: Mister Derrick!

DERRICK: Where's Otto?

HOUSEKEEPER: I don't know, but Mister Derrick!

DERRICK: Go get Otto!

HOUSEKEEPER: But...

DERRICK: I said.... What is it?

HOUSEKEEPER: Mister Derrick. Your offices. I saw from the window. They're on fire.

DERRICK: Fire?

HOUSEKEEPER: Yes, sir.

(DERRICK *looks at everyone. Goes to the gate, opens it; looks down the path. Suddenly sees the fire*)

DERRICK: Oh my God. The bell! Ring the bell! Fire!!!

VOICE: (*Off*) Fire!!! Fire!!! Fire!!!

(*Everyone runs out.* MAN *runs on.*)

MAN: Water!! Water!! Water!!

(MAN *runs off. Short pause.* RIP *enters on the path. His face is bruised and cut.*)

RIP: Water, I'd like some water.... (*Stumbles; looks into the garden*) Ho! Hello! (*Sees the coffee*) Ah! (*Fumbles to open the gate, enters the garden, approaches the coffee, then sees the breakfast*) Oh! Hello. (*Shuffles to the breakfast and begins to stuff food in his mouth. With his mouth full, not really calling.*) Hello? (*To himself*) Teeth hurt. (*Eats*) Water. (*Goes to coffee*) Huh. (*Pours coffee in his hand*) Hot! (*Drinks; goes back to the food, eats some more*)

(HEINRICH *enters on the path, coming from the direction of the fire. He carries a satchel. He limps. Sees* RIP. *Stops*)

HEINRICH: Morning.

RIP: *(Startled, scared)* What?!

HEINRICH: Morning.

RIP: *(Nods)* Yes, it's morning. *(Eats, though keeps glancing at* HEINRICH. *Pause)*

HEINRICH: Big fire. *(Points)*

RIP: Yes? Oh.

(Pause. HEINRICH *starts to open the gate.)*

RIP: Don't!

HEINRICH: *(Stops)* I'm looking for someone…. Is there anyone in the house I can talk to?

RIP: No.

(Pause)

HEINRICH: I guess everyone must be at the fire.

RIP: Yes.

HEINRICH: I'll come back then. *(Starts to leave)*

RIP: Wait!

*(*HEINRICH *turns back.)*

RIP: You don't want to knock me down?

HEINRICH: Why would I want to knock you down?

RIP: *(After a pause)* Come here come here come here come here.

(HEINRICH *enters the gate;* RIP *looks suspiciously around.)*

RIP: Tell me—is everyone mad here? Are you mad?

(HEINRICH *shakes his head.)*

RIP: Me neither. *(Whispers to* HEINRICH*)* They hit me.

HEINRICH: Who did?

RIP: They did. Look. *(Shows him his cuts)* I walk down from the mountains and I say— "hello", and a boy, he says "old man, who's your barber?" "Who's my what" I say and that's when I find this. *(Touches his beard)* Strange, isn't it? Where'd this come from?... And then I fall down—I don't know why—I haven't been drinking. And one boy—I like him—he says "give him a stick so he can stand up." "Thank you" I say. "Give him a kick so he can sit down" says the other boy and he kicks me. And I say "do you know where I live?" and another boy, I didn't see him 'til then, he says: "looks like he's been dead and dug up again." And he says: "has the circus come to town?" I say: "why do you say this to me?" And somebody kicks me. And I hurt. Why?

(HEINRICH *just looks at him. Pause*)

RIP: Sit down.

(HEINRICH *does.*)

RIP: What do you want?

HEINRICH: I'm looking for Meenie Derrick. Is this where she lives?

RIP: Who?

HEINRICH: Meenie Derrick.

RIP: Which one? That's two people. I know them both. There's Derrick and I don't know where he lives except where he always lives. And there's my Meenie and I don't know where she lives either except at home and I can't find that. Two people. Two heads.

HEINRICH: I was pointed in this direction. They said the white fence on Park Street.

RIP: *(To himself)* They got names for streets here?

HEINRICH: Though I could have got turned around. Everything seems very different than when I was last here.

RIP: For you too? We can be friends. One head. Water?

(HEINRICH *nods.*)

RIP: It's wash water. That's why it's brown. Usually I don't drink wash water but today I do. It's hot.

HEINRICH: It's coffee.

RIP: I smell. You live here?

HEINRICH: Did.

RIP: Me too. I think—me too. You been away?

HEINRICH: For almost ten years.

RIP: Only ten years? I been away for one night.

HEINRICH: I was in the war.

RIP: Ah, the war… What war?

HEINRICH: With the British. My regiment surrendered, and I was impressed as a seaman in His Majesty's Navy five years. I jumped ship in the Canary Islands. Caught a schooner. Came home. Who else lives here?

RIP: Who else?

HEINRICH: Besides yourself. Who takes care of you?

RIP: Nobody takes care of me. I don't live here.

HEINRICH: But you're in the garden. Who makes your food?

RIP: Don't know, I don't live here.

HEINRICH: But you're here.

RIP: So are you. Do you live here?

HEINRICH: Of course not. I just walked through the gate.

RIP: Me too. I walked in like you. One head. Hungry?

HEINRICH: Then you're not somebody's old grandfather they keep in the garden?

RIP: *(Smiles)* Come in, just like you… You going to knock me down now?

HEINRICH: No, but I think maybe I should knock. It looks sort of suspicious the two of us just walking into somebody's garden.... *(He gets up, starts to approach the house.)*

(SECRETARY runs out with an empty case.)

SECRETARY: *(Running out)* Mister Derrick! The safe! It's empty! It's been robbed!... *(Sees HEINRICH and RIP.)* Who are you? What do you want? *(Suddenly screams)* Thief! Thief!!

Scene Three

(Street in front of DERRICK's burning offices. Pump. Buckets. The fire off left. FIRST MAN at the pump.)

FOREMAN'S VOICE: *(Off)* Water!!!

FIRST MAN: *(Pumping)* Coming!!

SECOND MAN: *(Running in with buckets)* Keep pumping! Keep pumping!

FIRST MAN: I'm trying. Damn pump.

FOREMAN'S VOICE: *(Off)* Water!!!

FIRST MAN: *(To pump)* Get up! Get up!!!

SECOND MAN: *(Picks up one full bucket, waiting for another to be filled)* Harder! Pump harder!

FIRST MAN: It's not coming.

FOREMAN'S VOICE: *(Off)* Water!! Water!!

SECOND MAN: Use your muscles!!

FIRST MAN: I'm pumping. I'm telling you it's not coming up!!!

GRETCHEN: *(Running in with blankets)* Blankets! Blankets!

SECOND MAN: Pump! Pump!

FIRST MAN: You do it then!

FOREMAN'S VOICE: *(Off)* Water!!!

SECOND MAN: Damn it. *(Grabs the one bucket of water)* Coming! *(Runs out with bucket)*

GRETCHEN: Blankets! What do I do with the blankets??!!!

(THIRD MAN *runs in coughing, collapses choking.*)

FIRST MAN: *(To pump)* More! More! More!

THIRD MAN: *(Coughing)* I'm burning.

GRETCHEN: I've got the blankets now what do I do with them?!!!!!

FOREMAN'S VOICE: *(Off)* Water!

FIRST MAN: Coming!

GRETCHEN: Blankets! *(Suddenly looks up, screams.)* Ahhhhhhhhh!

(FIRST MAN *looks up.*)

FIRST MAN: The roof.

FOREMAN'S VOICE: *(Off)* The roof!!!

GRETCHEN: The roof! Back!!!!

FIRST MAN: Back.

FOREMAN'S VOICE: *(Off)* Back!!! The roof!!!!!

GRETCHEN: Ahhhhhhhhhhhhh!!!!!!!!!!!

(The roof has collapsed; silence.)

THIRD MAN: I'm burning up.

(FIRST MAN *just touches the pump and water comes out.*)

FIRST MAN: Now it comes. *(Pause; he takes a bucket to* THIRD MAN.*)* Here.

THIRD MAN: *(Throwing water on himself)* Thanks.

(Pause)

PART TWO

FIRST MAN: Now it comes.

(He walks off. DERRICK *enters, smeared with ash.)*

GRETCHEN: Senseless. *(Short pause)* Why? *(Short pause)* What do they want?

*(*DERRICK *just looks at the offices.)*

GRETCHEN: It makes you sick.

*(*DERRICK *nods.* CONSTABLE *and* SECRETARY *enter talking.)*

SECRETARY: One has a long white beard and the other—a limp. It's not likely that you'd lose them in a crowd.

CONSTABLE: Who said anything about a crowd? They're back in the hills with the rest of them. We've got dogs.

SECRETARY: They could be hiding in the cellar.

CONSTABLE: They *could* be on the moon. They are in the hills.

SECRETARY: Canucks?

CONSTABLE: You're not as stupid as you look.

GRETCHEN: But what do they want? I can understand robbing a safe, but torching a building?

CONSTABLE: They set the fire. You leave your house. So they can rob the safe. And escape.

SECRETARY: Simple.

CONSTABLE: And dumb. They picked the wrong town. Or the wrong constable. I'll find them. We'll track 'em and they'll lead us to the rest. We've got dogs. *(Starts to leave, stops.)* It's always this way, isn't it?

GRETCHEN: Which way?

CONSTABLE: From the outside. That's how you can catch it.

GRETCHEN: Catch what?

CONSTABLE: Disease. *(He leaves. Pause)*

SECRETARY: *(To* GRETCHEN*)* He's got dogs.

*(*FOREMAN *enters.)*

FOREMAN: *(To* DERRICK*)* He hasn't been seen since he left your house.

GRETCHEN: Who? *(Looks into* DERRICK*'s face)* No. Not Cockles?! That's not possible, Hans. You can't think, just because he took some… You don't really think…? Hans, he said they were Canucks!

DERRICK: *(To* SECRETARY*)* The safe, was it broken into or just open?

SECRETARY: Now that you mention it, Mister Derrick, it was open. But you can't think…? Maybe I should tell the constable. *(Starts to go)*

DERRICK: Otto. Leave the constable to worry about his dogs.

GRETCHEN: Hans you raised him!

DERRICK: I once raised pigs too. *(To* FOREMAN*)* The works. The northeast gate. Pull ten men and arm them. Keep them hidden. They'll try to sneak through there. Give the rest of the workers revolvers. But keep them working. Nothing should look out of the ordinary.

FOREMAN: Yes, sir. *(Leaves)*

DERRICK: *(To* SECRETARY*)* There's a Thomas Jones. A Sergeant Thomas Jones, he works at the Inn. You know who he is?

SECRETARY: Yes, sir.

DERRICK: Tell him I want to see him.

*(*SECRETARY *leaves.)*

DERRICK: He was the best Sergeant Major I had in the war. He can put together a little army within hours.

GRETCHEN: But Hans, the works? You don't think....

DERRICK: Even as a child, Cockles liked to play with fire. People don't change.

GRETCHEN: But how do you know it's Cockles?!!

DERRICK: I know. I know. *(Looks back at the fire)* Stupid bastard.

(DERRICK *and* GRETCHEN *leave.*)

Scene Four

(The hills. A clearing in the woods. JACK *up a tree, as a lookout,* FRANCIS *sits. A* BOY *fixes a shovel.)*

FRANCIS: Now what do you see?

JACK: More flame and more smoke.

FRANCIS: Good. They'll be watering ashes all night.... What's that you're doing, boy?

BOY: My father says, you fix your own tools, then you take good care of them.

FRANCIS: He's right, boy. He's.... How high the flames now?

JACK: Tall as three houses.

FRANCIS: Not high enough. Want 'em licking the clouds.

BOY: Why is that?

FRANCIS: 'Cause then our wives and fathers could see from over the hills, and they'd know we weren't flat drunk on our butts but doing what we said we'd do—gettin' our valley back. Tell me when they kiss the clouds, okay? *(To* BOY*)* Need some extra fingers?

BOY: No.

FRANCIS: Good boy. *(Pause)* What you see now, Jack?

JACK: Same as I saw the last time you asked.

FRANCIS: Oh. Must have built those offices with oak. 'Cause if it was pine you'd be seeing sparks too. See any sparks?

JACK: No.

FRANCIS: *(Nods)* Oak. *(Short pause)* Too bad. 'Cause no oak flame is going to reach the clouds. Looks like we'll have to wait for the works. Got to use powder with them as they're not wood but stone, so they won't burn but blast. My wife won't see it, but she'll hear it, I'll bet, 'cause the earth is going to shake when the works go up…. How you coming, boy?

BOY: Fine.

FRANCIS: Good boy.

(HENRY *enters.*)

HENRY: He's coming. He just crossed the stream.

FRANCIS: With a satchel?

HENRY: Two.

FRANCIS: Good. Good. Must have found a bank. Two satchels.

HENRY: How's it going down there, Jack?

FRANCIS: *(Laughs)* That's funny.

HENRY: What's funny?

FRANCIS: You say "down there", but you look up. That's funny.

JACK: It just keeps smoking, Henry. They must be pissin' in the coals.

HENRY: Let 'em piss, I say.

FRANCIS: Your boy, Henry, he's been fixing a shovel. Hasn't said boo, except when you ask him a question.

HENRY: Let me see, boy. *(Takes the shovel and smashes against the ground. Nothing happens. Smashes it again—the handle comes off.)* Good only for one bang, boy. That's not a shovel, that's a piece of straw. Try again, boy. Good for three bangs, that's a shovel, that's where I'll stop, so you'll know the next time. *(Hands him back the pieces)*

(BOY starts to fix the shovel again.)

FRANCIS: He's a good boy.

HENRY: That he is.

JACK: Oh! Oh!

FRANCIS: What, Jack?

JACK: It's the roof. The roof's fallen in.

FRANCIS: *(Laughs)* Good. Good. There won't be splinters left to pick their teeth with. Good.

(COCKLES enters with satchels.)

COCKLES: Where's the powder?

FRANCIS: Cockles, did you see? The roof's now the ground.

JACK: Climb up and see the picture, Cockles. It's such a lovely picture.

HENRY: A nice fire always warms the heart. Go watch.

COCKLES: If every building but one were on fire, I wouldn't stop to watch, I'd be too busy looking for a match to burn that one too.

HENRY: *(To BOY)* Yes. Yes. Frivolous to watch.

FRANCIS: Yes. Yes. Too busy to watch. I told Jack to come down, Cockles.

JACK: When did you tell me that? Cockles, he never told me that.

COCKLES: Where do you keep the powder?

FRANCIS: The powder? It's buried, of course. We're not stupid. Where'd we bury it, Henry?

COCKLES: Dig it up them. We're going to need it today.

FRANCIS: Today? We do the works today? We do two in one day?

COCKLES: They're like ticks, you got to keep squeezing them.

FRANCIS: Yes, like ticks. That's good. Also like fleas 'cause once they get on you they're hard to get off. Or like moths, 'cause they chew up and spit out everything you got. But ticks, that's good too.

HENRY: I don't know, Francis. The works, that's a lot for one day. I wouldn't want to be greedy.

FRANCIS: Who's being greedy, Henry. Think of it like this—we're locusts and we come to this valley. The offices, they were just breakfast, and a locust wouldn't leave a valley without having lunch, would he? And that's what the works is, lunch. Aren't you hungry for lunch, Henry?

HENRY: I'm hungry.

FRANCIS: Then let's say we're locusts and eat, Henry. And if we're locusts then we're not being greedy, but natural.

HENRY: I guess if you put it like that. Okay, Cockles, I'll eat the works.

COCKLES: Settled. We'll blast the works this afternoon.

HENRY: In the daylight?

FRANCIS: Of course. You don't eat lunch when it's dark, do you?

HENRY: No.

FRANCIS: Then what are you asking such a stupid question for?

PART TWO

COCKLES: *(Throwing down the satchels)* Here's all the money.

FRANCIS: I told 'em you found a bank.

COCKLES: The next best thing. It's from my uncle's safe. But there won't be any more. I'm coming with you.

FRANCIS: You? You want to be a farmer?

COCKLES: No. I mean, I want to be a part of your fight. This struggle. You can have my life. I won't disappoint you. That is, of course, if you want me.

HENRY: Yes. Yes.

COCKLES: Don't answer quite so quickly. You should know some things about me first. For four years I fought along side my Uncle, against the King and those like you Canucks who supported him. These hands may have killed one of your sons or a cousin or father. I sought to create a country, and to do that, I knew a great beast had to be killed. My hand was one of many which held the sword which severed his head. And when we won, I truly believed that a man would never again have to plow a straight furrow while glancing over his shoulder. He was to be left alone, his conscience better than a thousand laws. But the beast did not die, now not as one body but as many he lives—though each one smaller, like my Uncle.

HENRY: He's short? I've never seen him.

FRANCIS: I saw him once, but he was on a horse.

COCKLES: I mean less important.

HENRY: Not to me. He took our valley.

COCKLES: And we'll take his.

FRANCIS: Jack said we'd get two valleys.

COCKLES: A man becomes a believer but once in his life. You take away that belief and the rest is waiting to die. I still have my belief. I can help. Think it over.

(FRANCIS *and* HENRY *move away and whisper. Pause. Finally they return to* COCKLES.)

FRANCIS: With two satchels, we want you.

(JACK *makes a bird noise.*)

HENRY: What's he doing?

FRANCIS: I don't know. What are you doing, Jack?

JACK: That's the signal.

FRANCIS: What signal?

JACK: For someone coming.

FRANCIS: Hide. Hide.

(They run out. Pause)

(HEINRICH *enters pulling* RIP *along. Both out of breath)*

RIP: Stop pulling at me! Who are you? Who was that man that chased us? What did he want from us?

HEINRICH: Full of questions, aren't you?

RIP: I woke up. Walking so fast made me wake up. Where are we?

HEINRICH: Safe, I think.

RIP: Oh. Why did you drag me through that stream? There were stones. We could have walked on the stones.

HEINRICH: And who'd fish you out then?

RIP: Oh. Who are you?

HEINRICH: *(Looks around)* Sit.

(After a pause, RIP *sits.)*

HEINRICH: We'll stay here a while. Quiet.

RIP: Here. But not in here. *(Points to his head)* Loud in here.

(Pause)

HEINRICH: Not exactly how I imagined my homecoming.

RIP: Agree. Agree. Except I don't know where my home is, so I can't be coming home.... Tell me...

HEINRICH: More questions?

RIP: One. One... Am I mad?

HEINRICH: You've had a bad hit. Here, let me look at that bruise. *(Goes to* RIP*)*

RIP: I have symptoms. What I see I don't know. And what I know I don't see. There is a great gap.

(As HEINRICH *touches the bruise)*

RIP: Ahhh!

HEINRICH: That boy really gave you a good kick. Lie back and stretch out.

RIP: And then?

HEINRICH: And then rest. It's been a long walk. And I had to pull you along at quite a fast clip.

RIP: And then sleep?

HEINRICH: If you can. Yes. We should be safe here for a while.

RIP: *(Lies back)* I can, but I won't. *(Short pause)* I'm afraid to wake up. *(Short pause)* Either I am mad or the world is. But those two things are the same.... But for you too, everything is changed?

HEINRICH: Pretty much, old man.

RIP: Good. It's nice to have company.

HEINRICH: From the moment I got off the ship, I've been seeing it. It's like the war never happened, or maybe it happened all right, but they've buried it real good.

RIP: Ah, the war. An Indian war?

HEINRICH: The war with the British, old man; I already told you that.

RIP: Ah, that war. I don't know that war. One more thing I don't know. But who's counting.

HENRY: Everybody seems to be so busy. And everything's so clean.

RIP: Ah, clean. That is a sure sign of a madman. A madman is always clean. He washes at least ten times a day. So my Grandfather always said. That's why he never washed. Because he was sane. I smell. Will we stay the night?

HEINRICH: I don't know. Can you walk anymore?

RIP: I can walk. It's just that one night is a very long time. Anything can happen. *(Tries to get comfortable)* Wet. I have rheumatism. *(Short pause)* If I close my eyes will you become somebody else?

HEINRICH: Scared that I'll leave you? You're as safe here as anyplace else.

RIP: Oh. Then I'll rest. *(Pause. He laughs.)*

HEINRICH: What's funny?

RIP: I don't know. But I remember always laughing. I remember people always saying I was a happy man. I thought if I start to laugh I will remember what there is to laugh about. *(Laughs; stops)* Nothing. *(Closes his eyes)* Did you ever hear of a man whose name is Rip Van Winkle?

HEINRICH: Rip? Sure.

RIP: *(Sits up)* Yes?!

HEINRICH: When I was a boy, I knew Rip.

PART TWO

RIP: When you were a boy. Oh, must be another one... *(Lies down)* What was this Rip Van Winkle like?

HEINRICH: Rip, he was sort of the town drunk. Funny man, nice man, but a drunk.

RIP: Sounds like the same one. *(Short pause. Sits up)* What's become of Rip?

HEINRICH: What's become of him??? He's been dead for years.

RIP: Dead? *(Lies back down.)* Oh. *(Pause. Closes his eyes)* You won't leave me?

HEINRICH: Did I say I would?

RIP: Can I believe what you don't say?

(HEINRICH *open his satchel. Takes out first a handsome box, then reaches in and pulls out a canteen. Drinks)*

RIP: *(Opening his eyes)* What's that?

HEINRICH: Thirsty?

RIP: No. That. *(Points to the box)*

HEINRICH: Open it.

(Hands box to RIP, *who sits up and opens it)*

RIP: Razors? Is that what you do—cut throats? I have a throat. Is that why that man chased us?

HEINRICH: I'm a barber. Or was. That's how I earned my passage back here.... I was a barber in the army too. That's why I limp.

RIP: *(Lying back down.)* Makes sense.

HEINRICH: Does it?

RIP: Who cares anymore?

(Short pause)

HEINRICH: I was shaving a major. He falls asleep.

RIP: He what?

HEINRICH: Falls asleep.

RIP: Poor man.

HEINRICH: Bee stings him. He jumps up and his gun goes off. Shoots my foot.

RIP: Oh...I wake up. I'm walking down from the hills. I'm knocked down. I'm kicked in the head. I'm eating in a garden. I meet a man with a limp.... What's your name?

HEINRICH: Heinrich.

RIP: I know a Heinrich. *(Falling asleep)* Nice boy... I'm eating in a garden. I meet a Heinrich who has a limp. We're running away. I don't understand.... I don't understand...anything.... *(Pause)*

(HEINRICH *goes to* RIP, *waves his hand over his face—he is asleep. He packs his satchel.*)

HEINRICH: Sorry, old man, but I didn't travel three thousand miles to sit up here with you. And besides you've caused me enough trouble for one day.

(HEINRICH *hurries out.* BOY, COCKLES, FRANCIS, HENRY, *and* JACK *enter.*)

COCKLES: *(Looking over* RIP*)* Beast.

FRANCIS: He's a beast? He don't look like a beast.

COCKLES: Not him. The other one. There's a lesson for all of you. That's the kind of human beings they are. Drag the old up to the hills and leave 'em to die. Makes you sick. That's what we're fighting against.

FRANCIS: *(To the others)* Beasts.

(They nod.)

HENRY: *(To* BOY; *pointing in the direction of* HEINRICH*)* Beast.

JACK: What do we do with him? Might wake up and hear us, if we just leave him here.

PART TWO

FRANCIS: Jack is right.

BOY: I'll watch him.

JACK: You'll do that, boy?

BOY: Yes.

HENRY: Good boy. You watch him.

COCKLES: Now let's get the powder.

FRANCIS: Yes. The powder. Where did we bury it, Henry?

(They start to go.)

COCKLES: *(Leaving)* Now at the works. There's a gate. The northeast gate. We'll get in through there....

(They are gone. BOY *still with shovel, goes to* RIP. *He pushes* RIP *with his foot.)*

RIP: *(Waking up)* What? You've gotten smaller. I knew I shouldn't have gone to sleep.

BOY: Get up.

RIP: Are you the same one or somebody else?

BOY: Get up.

RIP: In a minute, son, you can't rush these bones.

(BOY hits RIP on the back with the shovel.)

RIP: Don't hit, son. Don't hit.

BOY: Get up.

(RIP slowly gets up.)

RIP: Are you taking me home? Did someone send you to take me home?

(BOY threatens RIP.)

RIP: Don't hit!

BOY: Can you use a shovel?

RIP: Who you want hit?

BOY: My father wants a hole dug. A shit hole.

RIP: A shit hole? Go dig it, son. I won't stop you.

(BOY *threatens* RIP.)

BOY: And you're going to dig it.

RIP: Me? Oh, I'm no good at digging shit holes, son. You ask anyone and they'll tell you, I'm a bad shit hole digger, son.

(BOY *threatens* RIP *again*)

RIP: Where do you want it?

BOY: Follow me.

RIP: I'm following. I'm following.

(BOY *and* RIP *leave.*)

Scene Five (a)

DERRICK: I am a cloud.

GUARD: A what, sir?

DERRICK: A cloud. To this ant, I'm a cloud. I'm also the wind. *(Blows on his hand)* It carries its food which is much bigger than it is, yet it doesn't appear to stumble. Strong.

GUARD: Yes, sir.

DERRICK: Through my palm, across my fingers—then onto the other palm and across my fingers—then back to the first palm and across those fingers. Sooner or later my hands will become the only world this ant remembers, and it will stop running and sit down and eat its food. Because here is the only home it's got.

(LOOKOUT *and* SGT JONES *enter.*)

SGT JONES: *(To* LOOKOUT*)* Tell the Colonel what you saw.

PART TWO

(DERRICK *lightly brushes off the ant.*)

LOOKOUT: Two men, sir. At least two men. Maybe three. They carry a barrel.

DERRICK: A barrel?

SGT JONES: Powder.

DERRICK: Yes.

LOOKOUT: I see 'em run down the steep side of this hill. Sort of slide down really on their backsides 'cause it's so steep, but they keep the barrel over their heads as they go down. They don't say nothing to each other. I thought I saw a third one at the top. They got rifles. They don't see me and I run back here.

SGT JONES: On their way to the works.

DERRICK: Yes. My foreman knows what to do. We'll squeeze them between the hills and the works. I'll cut them off at the north slope. You know the signal.

SGT JONES: I do, Colonel.

DERRICK: Then prepare yourself. *(Starts to leave)*

SGT JONES: Colonel. It'll be a turkey shoot.

(DERRICK *looks at him, nods slowly, then hurries off.* GUARD *who had left, now returns pushing* HEINRICH *before him.*)

GUARD: Sergeant, he was watching from those bushes.

HEINRICH: I didn't want to interrupt, are you from the town?

SGT JONES: Spy.

HEINRICH: Who's a spy? You don't think...? But a spy for what? The war is over! Look, my name is Heinrich Vedder. I grew up in this town. My regiment surrendered. For three years I was impressed in the British navy. I jumped ship....

SGT JONES: He's confessing. British sailor.

HEINRICH: I was impressed!

GUARD: (*Looking through satchel*) Razors.

HEINRICH: I'm a barber.

SGT JONES: Throat cutter. Tie him up.

HEINRICH: You're joking. Someone around here must know me. My name is Heinrich Vedder. I've come home.

(GUARD *grabs his wrists.*)

HEINRICH: What are you doing?

(GUARD *twists his wrists.*)

HEINRICH: Ahhhhhhh!!!!!!! What did I do? What did I do? (*Twists again*) Enough. Enough. Ahhhhhhhh!!!!!!! Stop!!!!!! Who are you…? What do you want? Someone must know who I am???!!!!

SGT JONES: He makes you weep, don't he? Get him out of my sight.

(*Distant gun shot*)

SGT JONES: Listen. That's the signal. Okay, boys! Attack!!!!!!!!

(LOOKOUT *and* SGT JONES *run out.*)

HEINRICH: (*Being pushed out by the* GUARD) My name is Heinrich Vedder.

GUARD: You think I care.

HEINRICH: I've come home.

GUARD: Lucky you. Move. Move. You've given me a headache.

(*They leave.*)

Scene Five (b)

(Another part of the woods. BOY *and* RIP *enter.* BOY *carries shovel,* RIP, *dirty from digging.)*

RIP: *(Entering)* I see what they mean when they say "dig your own grave". I got to rest now, son.

BOY: No.

RIP: What do you mean "no"? I said, I got to rest. Who's your father that lets you talk like to that me? *(Starts to sit)*

BOY: *(Threatens)* Don't.

RIP: How much more can I hurt. *(Starts to sit)*

BOY: *(Hits him)* Don't.

RIP: Why don't you go use that shit hole, now that it's dug.

*(*BOY *threatens* RIP.*)*

RIP: I think I have died and gone to hell and you are the devil. *(He looks around. He cries.)* Look at me, I'm crying, son. 'Cause I'm so lost. Don't you pity me?

BOY: *(Handing him the shovel)* Fix this.

RIP: The shovel? But the shovel's not broken.

*(*BOY *bangs the shovel on the ground. Bangs it again. On the third bang the handle comes off.)*

BOY: Fix it.

RIP: *(Taking the shovel)* You're a strange boy.

HENRY: *(Off. Yelling)* Boy! Boy! *(Runs on)* There you are, boy. Come with me. *(Grabs* BOY's *arm)* Come. Come. Hurry. Don't look back boy. We got to run. They're coming. Run. Run.

(They run out. COCKLES *runs in.)*

COCKLES: Henry! Henry! What happened?!!!! Stop! (*Shoots in the air. Short pause*) Stop. What happened?

RIP: The hole's finished.

COCKLES: What?

RIP: I said, the hole's finished. Can I sit down now?

(FRANCIS *runs in, starts to run off.*)

COCKLES: Francis!

(FRANCIS *stops.*)

FRANCIS: Quick! Quick! Come!

COCKLES: (*Grabs* FRANCIS) Francis, what happened?

FRANCIS: Awful. Jack's killed. They were waiting for us. They had guards. Hurry! No time!

COCKLES: (*Holding him.*) And the powder—what happened to it, Francis?

FRANCIS: They didn't get it. We tuck it against the wall. That's when they shoot Jack. Poor Jack. He was the lookout. And we run like hell. Come, come, they got men in the hills. We saw them. Come.

COCKLES: Why didn't you light it?!!

FRANCIS: Poor Jack. In the head. I hear them!!!! (*Tries to push* COCKLES *off*)

COCKLES: Give me that rifle.

FRANCIS: Take. Take. (*Pushes away from* COCKLES *and starts to run off*)

COCKLES: Francis. (*Points rifle at* FRANCIS)

FRANCIS: What are you doing?

COCKLES: Come with me. We can ignite that powder with one shot.

FRANCIS: No. No.

COCKLES: Which wall, Francis? By the gate? By the northeast gate?

FRANCIS: Yes. Yes. Where's Henry?

COCKLES: Gone. Like a jackrabbit.

FRANCIS: Me too. Me too. Like a rabbit. Let me go.

COCKLES: No, Francis. Please.

FRANCIS: *(Screams)* I hear them!!!!!!

(FRANCIS *turns to run,* COCKLES *shoots him.* RIP *moans.* COCKLES *looks at* RIP, *then turns away toward the works.*)

COCKLES: *(Walking off)* Burn. Burn.

(Pause)

RIP: *(Standing over* FRANCIS*)* Take my advice and don't wake up. *(He leaves.)*

Scene Five (c)

(Another part of the woods. DERRICK, CORPORAL, *and* LOOKOUT, *who has just entered.)*

DERRICK: *(To* LOOKOUT*)* And what does the Sergeant say?

LOOKOUT: They are routed, sir, like mice from their hole.

DERRICK: Dead?

LOOKOUT: Two, sir. One by us, and one without our help.

DERRICK: Any familiar faces?

LOOKOUT: They're Canucks, sir. We don't know any Canucks.

DERRICK: Of course.

(Distant gun shot)

DERRICK: Are we still firing?

LOOKOUT: That's not us. There's still one of 'em who fights or rather sort of fights, that is—he shoots, but not at us—only at the works.

DERRICK: The works?

LOOKOUT: He shoots once and then moves quickly. We've found blood so we think he's hit.

DERRICK: He moves where?

LOOKOUT: Toward us now. The Sergeant's behind him, pushing him in this direction, just as you'd stalk a wounded deer.

DERRICK: Tell the Sergeant to hold his ground, we'll deal with this one ourselves. Go. Hurry.

(LOOKOUT *leaves.*)

DERRICK: Corporal.

CORPORAL: Sir.

DERRICK: Take the men to the ridge and block any retreats.

CORPORAL: *(Starts to leave.)* And you, Colonel?

DERRICK: I'll be with you soon enough.

(CORPORAL *leaves. Gun shot, closer*)

DERRICK: Closer. Come to me, nephew. Sit on my lap, boy. I may still save your face. *(Leaves)*

Scene Five (d)

(Another part of the woods)

(COCKLES, *wounded, sits aiming rifle toward the works.*)

COCKLES: *(Shaking)* Steady. Steady. No! *(Grimaces)* Don't hurt. Wipe off face. *(Wipes off blood)* No blood. That's sweat, Cockles. Don't hurt. Steady. *(He shoots.)*

PART TWO

Oh. Again. Again. *(Grabs powder horn)* Fill. *(Drops horn)* Don't spill! *(Scoops up powder)* Not wet. Steady. Fill. Eyes burn. Steady. Now hit the barrel. Which barrel? I see two. Pick one, Cockles. You picked one? *(Shakes his head)* Aim. Aim. Don't shake!!!! There. *(Pulls trigger—nothing)* No? Wet? Try again. Aim. *(Pulls trigger—nothing)* No? No!!!! Oh, forgot to load. *(Laughs)* Dumb. Here. Here. I load. *(Puts in a bullet)* I load. Ha ha. Aim. Aim. *(Cries)* What's this? I got sweat in my eyes. Don't sweat. I'm shaking!!!! Aim. Two barrels. Aim. *(Shoots)* No blast. Load! Load! Load!

(COCKLES *stops, breaks down crying.* DERRICK *enters.* COCKLES *feels his presence and quickly turns around.*)

COCKLES: Oh, load! Load!

DERRICK: *(Slaps his face)* Fly. Got him.

(Pause)

COCKLES: *(Turns towards the works)* Blast. Blast.

DERRICK: Get up, boy. They don't know you're a part of all this. And you think I want them to find out? Wouldn't look good, boy. Get up. Up.

(COCKLES *cries.*)

DERRICK: I have pity for you. No one will ever know.

(Slowly COCKLES *gets up.)*

COCKLES: *(Holding up his hands)* Shaking.

DERRICK: Yes. I know. I know.

(DERRICK *stabs* COCKLES *in the chest. He falls and dies.* DERRICK *takes off* COCKLES's *jacket, bunches it up and throws it in the woods.* RIP *enters without being seen. He watches.* DERRICK *takes his knife and carves off* COCKLES's *face. Blood.* RIP *stares.*)

DERRICK: *(To the body)* I'll say you went to Europe. No one will know. *(He drags the body out.)*

(RIP *watches them off. Pause*)

RIP: Wrong. Wrong.

Scene Six

(The Garden. Early evening. Chairs, etc. as in Scene Two. MEENIE *and the* SCHOOLTEACHER *enter from the house.)*

SCHOOLTEACHER: October.

MEENIE: But that's three months away!

SCHOOLTEACHER: September then.

MEENIE: I mean, that's too soon. June. Maybe early June.

SCHOOLTEACHER: But why should we wait so long? Late October then.

MEENIE: What if you changed your mind? I want to give you time to change your mind.

SCHOOLTEACHER: It won't change. Late October.

MEENIE: But I've so much to learn. You'll be bored with me in a week. I'll guarantee you that.

SCHOOLTEACHER: I won't be bored. Middle of October.

MEENIE: You're going backward!

SCHOOLTEACHER: November then.

MEENIE: April. Very, very late April. Maybe father will send me to New York and I'll see things there and I won't be so boring. It'll take you at least two weeks to get sick of me if I've been to New York.

SCHOOLTEACHER: The middle of November. November's a good month for a wedding.

MEENIE: March.

SCHOOLTEACHER: December and we can go to New York together.

PART TWO

MEENIE: February. And I'll read a hundred books between now and then.

SCHOOLTEACHER: January because there's only eighty books worth reading.

MEENIE: No. Too cold. Too cold. We'd be stuck inside then, and you'd really see how boring I am.

SCHOOLTEACHER: I can see that there's no point in talking to you today. I'll go get the books you want. You want to come?

MEENIE: No, I'll wait.

SCHOOLTEACHER: I won't be long.

(GRETCHEN *enters from the house.*)

SCHOOLTEACHER: Mrs Derrick.

GRETCHEN: James.

MEENIE: Let's go, James.

SCHOOLTEACHER: I thought you weren't coming.

MEENIE: I'll walk with you as far as the blacksmith's. I feel like getting out of the house.

(HOUSEKEEPER *has entered from behind* GRETCHEN.)

HOUSEKEEPER: Wait 'til she has children of her own.

(GRETCHEN *nods, obviously hurt.* SECRETARY *runs in from the path.*)

SECRETARY: They're back! They've just come back!

GRETCHEN: My husband?!

SECRETARY: It'll take more than the Canucks to bring down the colonel.

GRETCHEN: Hans! *(Starts to go, stops)* And...and Cockles???

SECRETARY: Gone.

HOUSEKEEPER: Gone?

SECRETARY: The colonel said he booked a seat on the morning coach. Told somebody he was going abroad.

GRETCHEN: Who?

SECRETARY: Somebody. I guess the engagement hurt him more than we thought. I mean, to run away like that.

GRETCHEN: Yes… Thank God they're back. Hans…! *(She runs off.)*

SECRETARY: They've got prisoners too.

HOUSEKEEPER: Canucks?

SECRETARY: No, Baptists. Of course Canucks! Three. And a boy.

HOUSEKEEPER: A boy? They brought a boy with them?

SECRETARY: Killed three more. One of the bodies, I saw it myself. It had no face.

HOUSEKEEPER: What do you mean, no face?

SECRETARY: What do you think? He had no face. They carved off his face. That's what Canucks do, you know. They're very superstitious. They carve off the face and then they think it's all right.

(Servant GIRL runs in from the house.)

HOUSEKEEPER: *(Stopping her)* Where are you going?

GIRL: To the square. I just saw from the window, Mister Derrick's giving a speech! Most of the town's there already!

HOUSEKEEPER: *(To GIRL)* You stay here.

GIRL: What? Why?

HOUSEKEEPER: Someone has to. Hurry.

(HOUSEKEEPER and SECRETARY hurry out.)

GIRL: It's not fair!

PART TWO

(Sulking, she starts to walk back to the house. GUARD *enters with* BOY, HEINRICH, HENRY, *and* RIP, *as prisoners, their hands tied, all tied to one piece of rope.* RIP *is the only one gagged.)*

HEINRICH: *(Quietly)* I saw her!

GUARD: Shut up!

GIRL: Oh! Oh! *(She is frightened, stands behind a chair.)*

GUARD: If it was up to me, I'd be dragging all of you along by your throats. So don't tempt me. Get! *(He pushes them through the gate.)* Excuse us, miss, but it's the colonel's orders. I'll see to it that these gentlemen mind their manners.

GIRL: Are they…?

GUARD: Canucks? *(She nods.)* That they are, miss. Beasts in human flesh. *(To prisoners)* Let me see. *(Tests the wind)* Yeh, this is a good place. Down wind. Now sit! *(He pushes them down. To* GIRL, *rubbing his hands.)* A dirty business, isn't it?

GIRL: Can I get you something to drink?

GUARD: Cold. Anything cold.

*(*GIRL *leaves.)*

GUARD: *(Looking after her)* Good buns. Now you boys watch yourselves, I see you getting it up and I'll lop it off. *(He goes to the fence, looks down the path.)*

HEINRICH: *(Whispers)* She's here! I saw her!

HENRY: Who?

HEINRICH: Meenie!

HENRY: *(To* BOY*)* I guess we're supposed to know who Meenie is. Do you, boy?

BOY: *(Shakes his head)* Good rope. Could have used this to fix the shovel.

(RIP *tries to talk through the gag.*)

HENRY: What's he saying, boy?

BOY: *(Listens)* He's saying, he's been here.

HENRY: Ah, is that good or bad?

(GIRL *enters with drink.*)

GIRL: Can you see Mister Derrick speaking?

GUARD: Just backs of heads. *(Takes drink)* Thank you, miss.

GIRL: Should I get something cold for... *(Points to prisoners)*

GUARD: If you have blood, miss.

GIRL: Blood??! Is that what they drink?

GUARD: I wouldn't be surprised.

GIRL: Think of it.

GUARD: It's a strange world, miss.

GIRL: And the old man, is he their leader? Is that why he's gagged?

GUARD: If the one who talks the most is their leader then he's the leader all right.

GIRL: What does he talk about?

GUARD: Mostly nonsense, miss. I think he's mad.

GIRL: Their leader's mad?

GUARD: Seems logical to me, miss.

GIRL: Do you think I could hear him say something?

GUARD: I'm not sure if....

GIRL: Oh please! Nobody ever lets me see anything I want to see!

GUARD: Well, I guess there's no harm in it.... As long as you stay back. Remember—beasts.

PART TWO

GIRL: Yes. Yes.

(GUARD *goes to* RIP *takes off his gag.* RIP *just looks at him.*)

GUARD: Come on old man, don't embarrass me. *(Short pause)* Say something mad. *(Short pause)* Speak! *(Kicks him)*

RIP: Wrong. Wrong.

GUARD: There. Here it comes.

GIRL: Oooh!

RIP: Tear it down. I've seen hell and it is blood on a head. Bury. Bury. Where is my shovel? I want to dig. Get away. Hurry. The world has been carved faceless. Run and get away. Die once and be happy. Do not go asleep. Do not dream. Do not lie in wet grass even for one night. Tear it down. I know. And the fields will grow and have a face again and I will know where I am. Look. Look. I have eyes and I see bad. Bad and wrong. I don't know anything but I know it is wrong. Gut and level and drive to the dogs, that would be a start. I can see and I say stop. Stop! Wrong and not right and not good. Bad, I say, and awful. Put away all knives. Put them into your chests. I have moss on my chin. It grows. Do not shave my face, but let the weeds grow. Where is my shovel so I can dig and have moles in my stomach and worms for my fingers and let ants scratch my itch. Ants, they were not meant to have faces. They are the lucky ones. Have I convinced you? I must. I must. Because we must all band together and kill each other. Her too. Her too. Because she is young. And him. *(The* GUARD*)* Kill him.

GUARD: That's enough, old man.

RIP: Kill him so he may feed the sun. I have dug the shit hole. Take me there and let me jump. I want to help a tree. Plant. Plant. And then lie down and feed the seed. Breath. Let's have breath and let it be the wind. The sun has eyes and the moon a mouth, that is face enough. Let them live, let us die.

GUARD: I said, that's enough. (*He is getting worried.*)

RIP: You're right. That is enough. We are too much. So let's tear us down! (*Screams*) Where is my shovel?!!!!

GUARD: Take it easy.

RIP: Take me home!!!! Take me home!!!!

GUARD: (*Trying to gag him*) Shut up!

RIP: Wrong. Wrong. Wrong.

GUARD: Don't bite!

RIP: Wrong!!!!!

(GUARD *beats him across the head.* RIP *collapses—knocked out. Pause.* GUARD *rubs his bit hand.*)

GIRL: He gives you the chills…. Let me see. Bleeding. Come inside. We'll clean it out.

(GUARD *hesitates, then starts to go, turns back and forces a laugh. They leave.*)

HEINRICH: (*To* BOY) Pull. Pull you rope. Tight. Come on. Hurry.

HENRY: Do as he says, boy.

HEINRICH: Good. Not that tight! There. Like that. Keep it like that. (*Tries to untie knot with his teeth.*) It's coming. It's… No loosen. Just a bit. Little more. There. (*He unties the knot, begins to free his hand, hears someone coming.*) Relax! Relax! (*He hides his hand and face—pretends to be asleep.*)

(HOUSEKEEPER *and* SECRETARY *enter, talking.*)

HOUSEKEEPER: A party! That's easy enough for him to say. But who's going to cook?

SECRETARY: Victory deserves its celebration.

HOUSEKEEPER: I haven't even shopped today.

SECRETARY: Relax. The girl will help.

HOUSEKEEPER: She'll help me to my grave. *(Passing by the prisoners)* Look at them.

SECRETARY: Animals.

(HOUSEKEEPER and SECRETARY exit into the house. HEINRICH waits for them to go, then quickly stands up.)

HEINRICH: Sh-sh. *(He sneaks off.)*

HENRY: *(Trying to bite his rope)* How did he do that boy? Pull, boy. *(The rope gets tighter.)* That hurts. Don't pull like that, boy, pull like you did for him. *(Gets tighter.)* Is that how you pulled when he said pull? Try again, boy. Oh, it hurts, boy. *(His hands have been pulled tight together in front of his face.)* That man must have teeth like a dog. This isn't going to work, boy.

BOY: *(Shakes his head)* No.

HENRY: *(Looks at BOY)* You're a good boy.

(GRETCHEN and SGT JONES enter, they are followed at a distance, by DERRICK and MEENIE. GRETCHEN keeps turning back to glance at DERRICK and MEENIE.)

SGT JONES: *(Entering)* Quite the speaker. That's the colonel for you. You should have seen him at Saratoga. What a speech.

GRETCHEN: *(Turning back)* Hans?

MEENIE: *(Pulling at his sleeve)* Father, I thought you were just wonderfully handsome up there.

(He pats her head.)

MEENIE: So now tell me just one reason why I can't.

DERRICK: Why you can't what?

MEENIE: Go to New York!

DERRICK: I don't know why you can't, Meenie.

MEENIE: Then I can?!

DERRICK: And I don't know why you can go. Meenie, I don't think this is the time.

MEENIE: It's never the time!

DERRICK: Meenie...

GRETCHEN: Hans?

MEENIE: Don't you butt in, he's talking to me!

DERRICK: Don't shout at your mother.

GRETCHEN: Hans, don't...

SGT JONES: I never heard anything like it.

(HEINRICH *has returned—unnoticed. He stares at* MEENIE.)

SGT JONES: Then you should have heard him at Ridgefield.

DERRICK: *(To* MEENIE*)* I don't know what's the matter with you two.

MEENIE: Ask her!

SGT JONES: The gift of words. Some of us have it, and some of us...well, look at me. *(He sits.)* Is there any sherry?

DERRICK: Meenie, get the sergeant some sherry.

MEENIE: Let her get it! Or maybe you don't trust her.

GRETCHEN: I'll go.

(GIRL *and* HOUSEKEEPER *enter with some plates.*)

GIRL: *(Entering)* I wasn't holding his hand, he has a cut!

DERRICK: Gretchen, I don't think you should take orders from your daughter.

GIRL: You don't believe me do you?!

GRETCHEN: I'll go. We'll talk later. *(She starts to leave.)*

SGT JONES: Talk. Talk. Talk. That man's got the gift from God.

PART TWO

HOUSEKEEPER: Then he could have talked to me and found out we didn't have enough food!

GIRL: *(Suddenly drops a plate)* You have a lot of nerve to call me a liar!!

DERRICK: *(Yells)* What is wrong with everybody?!!!!!!

(Pause)

MEENIE: *(Turns, suddenly sees HEINRICH)* Heinrich?

HEINRICH: Meenie?

GRETCHEN: Oh God. Oh God. He's alive.

(HEINRICH starts to move toward MEENIE. GUARD and SECRETARY enter talking.)

SECRETARY: I think two of 'em are the ones I ran off this morning....

MEENIE: I don't believe it! Heinrich!!!

(MEENIE holds open her arms. GUARD turns and sees HEINRICH, reaches for his gun.)

GUARD: Stop!!!!

(GUARD shoots HEINRICH, who falls. MEENIE screams.)

GRETCHEN: Why did you shoot him?!

(Others run to HEINRICH.)

DERRICK: He's breathing. Help me get his shirt off. Otto, get the doctor. We'll bring Heinrich to his office. Run!

(SECRETARY runs out.)

SGT JONES: *(To GUARD)* Take his legs.

GUARD: I thought he was going to hurt her.

SGT JONES: Take his legs!!

(GUARD and SGT JONES pick him up.)

DERRICK: Careful. Keep his head up.

(SCHOOLTEACHER *enters with books.*)

SCHOOLTEACHER: What's happened here?

GUARD: *(As they carry him off)* He's a Canuck, isn't he?

DERRICK: Hurry. Hurry!

(They carry him off. DERRICK *follows.)*

SCHOOLTEACHER: Meenie.

MEENIE: Get away! Get away!

SCHOOLTEACHER: Meenie, what is it?

MEENIE: *(Hugging* GRETCHEN*)* Mother, it's Heinrich.

GRETCHEN: I know, dear. Come. Let's hurry.

(They leave.)

SCHOOLTEACHER: *(To* HOUSEKEEPER*)* Who is it?

HOUSEKEEPER: The Vedder boy, Heinrich.

SCHOOLTEACHER: Meenie's Heinrich?

*(*GIRL *nods.)*

SCHOOLTEACHER: But he was dead.

HOUSEKEEPER: Maybe is, but he wasn't.

*(*GIRL *and* HOUSEKEEPER *hurry off.)*

SCHOOLTEACHER: *(Nods to himself)* Oh. *(Sits on the fence, facing upstage. He nods to himself again. Pause)*

HENRY: Don't pull, boy. I think I'll stay put right here.

*(*RIP *groans, begins to wake up.)*

RIP: Hurt. Hurt. My head. Feels like someone's been playing drums on my head. Ow! ...What a dream I had. No, Rip, that weren't a dream, that was a nightmare. *(Tries to move his hands)* What's this? Now who would do something like that? Must be somebody's joke. Maybe little Heinrich. I used to do the same thing to my Grandpa when he was sleeping, I'd tie his shoes.... Ow, I do hurt.... *(Turns)* Where????

PART TWO

...No, no, that was a dream. You've been sleeping, Rip. Wait a minute, now I remember—there was that queer fellow with the keg. This must be his valley. *(Finally notices* BOY *and* HENRY*)* Who???? ...Must be friends of that queer fellow. *(Looks around.)* You see my rifle? I had it with me when I come up the hill. What a rain that was. Never seen it rain like that. *(To* BOY*)* You look sort of familiar. But you boys all look alike at your age. I guess, that's it. Or maybe I've seen you playing with little Heinrich. *(Pause, then pats his chest)* Let me see. I got it here.... Be easier if somebody'd untie my hands. *(Struggles as he reaches into his pocket, pulls out the paper)* ...look here. All yellow. Must be the dampness. Here, boy, read this to me. I'd like to hear it said once again.

*(*BOY *shakes his head.)*

RIP: No? Why not, boy? Read it like Heinrich reads it.

*(*BOY *shakes his head.)*

RIP: Can't you read, boy?

*(*BOY *shakes his head.)*

RIP: Oh, I'm sorry for you, boy.

(Looks at HENRY, *shakes his head, and turns to* SCHOOLTEACHER. HENRY *shakes his head.)*

RIP: Hey you! You over there on the fence!

*(*SCHOOLTEACHER *turns around.)*

RIP: That's right—you! Can you read?

SCHOOLTEACHER: I'm a schoolteacher.

RIP: A schoolteacher! That's even better than Heinrich. Come here come here come here...

*(*SCHOOLTEACHER *hesitates.)*

RIP: I said, come here.

*(*SCHOOLTEACHER *approaches.)*

RIP: This. Read this. *(Hands him the paper)* Now we're going to hear a schoolteacher read it. No—out loud. So I can hear it too.

SCHOOLTEACHER: "Know all men by these presents that I, Rip Van Winkle, in consideration for sums received do hereby sell and convey to Mister Hans Derrick all my estate, houses, lands whatsoever whereof he now holds possession by mortgaged deeds from time to time executed by me." Where did you get this?

RIP: Where? Derrick and my whore they try to get me to sign it. But I don't.

SCHOOLTEACHER: *(Starts to run out)* Mister Derrick! Mister Derrick!

RIP: Where you going with my paper?!

(DERRICK *and* GRETCHEN *enter; talking.*)

DERRICK: *(Entering)* …it's lodged in the chest. So there's still a chance….

SCHOOLTEACHER: Mister Derrick, read this!

DERRICK: What is it?

SCHOOLTEACHER: Read it!

DERRICK: *(Reads)* Where did you get this?

(SCHOOLTEACHER *nods toward* RIP.)

GRETCHEN: What is it, Hans? Give it to me. Give it!

(DERRICK *stares at* RIP, GRETCHEN *reads.*)

DERRICK: *(Approaching* RIP*)* Who are you?

RIP: Me? Everybody knows me…I'm Rip Van Winkle.

(GRETCHEN *screams and faints.*)

DERRICK: Water! Water!

RIP: I'd like some water.

BOY: Who's Rip Van Winkle?

HENRY: Hell if I know.

Scene Seven

(The Garden. Evening. BOY *is curled up asleep—untied.* HENRY *is passed out in a chair. Remnants of food and drink around. Pause.* GIRL, HOUSEKEEPER, *and* SECRETARY *enter.)*

HOUSEKEEPER: Hurry. Going to rain.

(They start to clean up.)

SECRETARY: And then?

GIRL: Nosey, aren't you?

SECRETARY: Can I help it if I had to stay at the doctor's?! So what happened then?!!!

GIRL: Mister Van Winkle—well, you could tell he was a little….

SECRETARY: A little what?

GIRL: *(To* HOUSEKEEPER*)* Confused?

HOUSEKEEPER: That he was.

GIRL: Confused. He just stood there….

SECRETARY: Where?

GIRL: There by the fence. He just stood there and Mister Derrick, he says "Rip?" and Mister Van Winkle says: "Derrick?", and Mrs Derrick or Mrs Van Winkle she's drinking water now and she says: "Rip?" and he says, he says….

SECRETARY: What?!

GIRL: He says: "Whore".

SECRETARY: Really? Why?

GIRL: *(Shrugs)* And Meenie, she's here by now, and she says, "Father?" and Derrick, he says, "What?" and

Mister Van Winkle says, "Meenie?" and it goes on like that for quite a while.

(SECRETARY *nods.*)

HOUSEKEEPER: Did you see his face?

SECRETARY: Whose face?

HOUSEKEEPER: Derrick's face.

GIRL: *(Nods)* Chalk.

SECRETARY: No.

GIRL: Yes. And later, after Mister Van Winkle was told where he was and everything that had happened, then he cried.

SECRETARY: Mister Van Winkle?

GIRL: No, Mister Derrick. And so did Mrs Derrick or Mrs Van Winkle. They both cried. That was after Mister Van Winkle said he was going to pull down the works and farm his land.

SECRETARY: Pull down the works?!!!

GIRL: And farm his land. That's when he cried, because he said those works, that was his life, and that was the life of this whole valley, but he just said if what I've seen today, you call a life, then we'd all be better off being dead, so I'm going to start all over and pull them down.

SECRETARY: *(To* HOUSEKEEPER*)* He said that?

HOUSEKEEPER: He's saying that, yes. And he's saying, we're going to be farmers from now on, and we're not going to hurry 'cause you can't hurry a harvest, you got to learn to wait, so there'll be no hurrying anymore....

GIRL: And Mister Derrick says, "You can't destroy it"; he says, "It won't work", and he holds his face.

PART TWO

HOUSEKEEPER: And Mister Van Winkle says, "It will work with me as the boss". You should have been there.

GIRL: I wouldn't have missed it for anything. My favorite was when Mister Van Winkle, he looks at Meenie and he says, "How much you've grown in one night".

SECRETARY: In one night?!

GIRL: Yes. And that's what Meenie and Derrick and Mrs Van Winkle or Mrs Derrick said too, "one night?" Just like you said it, they say, "One night?!" And then the Schoolteacher, he was there though no one was paying much attention to him he was there and he says, "But you've been away fifteen years". And Mister Van Winkle he says: "fifteen years?" And then he looks up at the sky.

HOUSEKEEPER: He looks up at the mountains.

GIRL: No, it was the sky.

HOUSEKEEPER: The mountains.

GIRL: The sky and he just shakes his head.

SECRETARY: Seems like everybody was shaking their heads.

GIRL: Me too. You couldn't help it. It was miracle after miracle. You should have been there.

HOUSEKEEPER: Yes.

GIRL: Now tell us about Heinrich.

SECRETARY: He'll live. *(He leaves.)*

HOUSEKEEPER: Hurry. Going to rain.

(They start to leave with the plates, etc. RIP enters from the house, passing them. They nod. RIP is clean shaven, wearing clean clothes. He strolls along, picks up a bottle. Pause. Then he suddenly smashes the bottle.)

RIP: *(Softly)* Enough.
(Thunder and lightning)
RIP: Enough.
(Thunder and lightning)

                END OF PART TWO

PART THREE
"SOBER"

Scene One

(A section of a field, near a road. Fifteen years later)

(Farmers work the field: JUDITH *and* DUTCH *upstage with hoes;* JONATHAN *and* RICHARD *down left with picks;* CLYDE *and* EDWARD *center with a plow—*CLYDE *pulls;* EDWARD *guides. Very hot. They are exhausted. The earth is dust.)*

CLYDE: Push! Just push, can you do that?!

EDWARD: What do you think I'm doing?!

CLYDE: Well, I don't think you're pushing! Push! Push!

EDWARD: I am! I am!

RICHARD: You getting anywhere? All I'm doing is making cracks.

JONATHAN: Could plop the seeds in the cracks, then spit in the cracks. Might seem like rain to a seed.

RICHARD: I think these cracks go to China. Think the whole earth's suddenly become rock.

JONATHAN: Got to rain sooner or later.

RICHARD: Who says?

JONATHAN: Always has. These fields fed us good up to now.

RICHARD: Last year's not this year.

JONATHAN: Have to learn to eat dust then.

RICHARD: Or learn not to eat.

CLYDE: You pushing? I ask you, if you're pushing?!

EDWARD: I'm not talking.

CLYDE: Then you better be pushing.

EDWARD: I'm having a cup of tea. What do you think I'm doing?!!! I'm pushing!!!

CLYDE: Must be a stone then.

EDWARD: No stone, that's the ground.

CLYDE: I said, it must be a stone then! Look! Look!!

EDWARD: Don't go blaming me. What I do?

CLYDE: It's what you're not doing. Look!

EDWARD: I'm looking!!! *(Checks for a rock under the plow)* I don't know what you're yelling at me for.

CLYDE: It's hot.

EDWARD: It's hot for me too.

JUDITH: Hot.

DUTCH: *(Hoe breaks in his hands.)* No. Broke.

JUDITH: Dutch?

(DUTCH drops the hoe, falls to his knees.)

JUDITH: Dutch?!

DUTCH: Broke.

EDWARD: No stone. No stone.

CLYDE: There is! There is!!

RICHARD: *(Looking off)* Fight. Fight!

JONATHAN: Who?

RICHARD: Can't see.

EDWARD: Fight?

PART THREE

RICHARD: In the next field. Can't see who.

CLYDE: Fight?

JUDITH: Fight?

RICHARD: Three of them.

CLYDE: Three fights?

RICHARD: Men. Men.

DUTCH: Fight?

JUDITH: Yes. Yes.

RICHARD: *(Shouting:)* Fight! Fight! Fight!

(RIP *runs in; he uses a cane now.*)

RIP: What's happening? What are you shouting about? Why aren't you working?

RICHARD: There's a fight, Rip.

RIP: *(Looks off)* A fight? What about?

RICHARD: The heat must have got them.

RIP: The devil's what's got them! Stop them! *(Turns back)* Keep working. Work! We got a crop to plant! *(Runs off)* Stop them!

GEORGE: *(Running in)* Rip! Rip!

(RIP *runs back in.*)

RIP: What is it?! Look—they're fighting.

GEORGE: *(Points behind him)* And they're quitting.

RIP: What?

GEORGE: They're just leaving their plows and walking away.

RIP: Why? Why?

GEORGE: They just are.

RIP: I'll talk to them. I'll talk. Quick.

(GEORGE *and* RIP *run off.*)

JONATHAN: To join Derrick, is why they're quitting.

RICHARD: You think?

CLYDE: Derrick????

JONATHAN: Don't you know?

CLYDE: What? What?

JONATHAN: One dollar a week.

CLYDE: What's one dollar a week?

JONATHAN: That's what they're going to pay. One dollar a week.

CLYDE: Who?

RICHARD: I heard two dollars a week.

JONATHAN: Two dollars a week?

RICHARD: At least.

EDWARD: You think they're going to pay two dollars a week?

CLYDE: Who?!

RICHARD: How much you make now?

CLYDE: Thirty cents a week.

RICHARD: Make that in one morning at the works.

CLYDE: The works? What works?

EDWARD: Don't you know?

CLYDE: What? What?

RICHARD: Derrick's going to start up the old works.

CLYDE: No.

EDWARD: He didn't know.

CLYDE: When?

JONATHAN: As soon as Rip decides to sell it to him.

CLYDE: Why won't he?

PART THREE

EDWARD: He will.

JONATHAN: He will?

EDWARD: For ten thousand dollars.

CLYDE: For ten thousand dollars?!!

JONATHAN: Where did you hear that?

RICHARD: He wants to move to Paris.

EDWARD: To London.

RICHARD: To London? I thought it was Paris.

EDWARD: To London.

RICHARD: To London? Really? Where did you hear that?

CLYDE: And what about us, while he's spending his ten thousand dollars in London? What are we supposed to do?

JONATHAN: I've heard a rumor.

RICHARD: A rumor? A rumor about what?

JONATHAN: You haven't heard?

RICHARD: What? What?

JONATHAN: That Derrick just might take the works by force.

RICHARD: Where did you hear that?

EDWARD: So that's why they went to see him.

RICHARD: Who went to see who?

EDWARD: The postmaster and a couple of others. They must have gone to Derrick to plead with him not to use force.

JONATHAN: They'll never convince him. The real question is—can he control his men.

RICHARD: Men? He has men?

JONATHAN: If you're going to take a works by force then you've got to have men. Don't be stupid.

CLYDE: How many men does he have?

RICHARD: I'd say a hundred would be a reasonable estimate, unless one of you knows something I don't.

JONATHAN: No, no, a hundred sounds about right.

CLYDE: No, we don't know anything you don't know.

(RIP *returns, upset, shouting to all the fields.*)

RIP: Get back! Get back into the fields! This is no time to run! Come back and work. God gave us the strength to work! This drought is our test! It will rain! It will!

(CLYDE *makes a move to leave.*)

RIP: Where are you going?! (*Grabs* CLYDE) We are farmers, we belong in the fields! (*Throws him down*) Look up! Look up and pray! This is our trial! (*Falls onto his knees. Sings:*)
We gather together
To ask the Lord's blessing.
He chastens and hastens,
His will to make known.
Sing!
So from the beginning,
The fight we are winning,
Sing praises to His Name,
He forgets not His….

(RIP *collapses. Pause.* GEORGE *runs in.*)

GEORGE: Rip! Rip! Wake up! Wake up!!! …Somebody help me. (*No one moves.*) We'll take him to the nearest house. It's just the heat. Help me! Help!!!!!!

(EDWARD *slowly moves to help.*)

PART THREE

GEORGE: Take his shoulders. And watch his head. Keep it up. I said, watch his head! It'll be all right, Rip. It's the heat. It's hot. It's hot.

(They carry RIP off. Pause)

JONATHAN: You think he'll come?

RICHARD: Derrick?

(JONATHAN nods.)

RICHARD: I don't think it's a question of if, but when. And I'd say, the sooner the better.

JONATHAN: Well you won't find me standing in the middle of the road trying to stop him.

RICHARD: With a hundred men on horseback charging down from the hills, you'd have to be crazy not to stay locked in your own house.

CLYDE: They have horses?

RICHARD: I wouldn't be surprised.

(Throws down his pick. They start to leave.)

CLYDE: It's a shame.

JONATHAN: *What is?*

CLYDE: After all Rip's done for this valley.

JONATHAN: Last year's not this year.

(They go.)

JUDITH: Did you hear that, Dutch? Maybe we should get our gun out.

(DUTCH pours out a little bottle onto the ground.)

JUDITH: What are you doing, Dutch?

DUTCH: Making the ground soft.

JONATHAN: But there's only so much water. You're supposed to save it, so you can drink it, Dutch.

DUTCH: It's not water.

JUDITH: No?

DUTCH: It's piss.

Scene Two

(Outside DERRICK's *shack in the hills. Bench. Stool. Table. Dogs bark.)*

*(*DERRICK *sits at a table, writing. He is dressed as a goat shepherd.)*

(Pause)

(Mad SHEPHERD *enters with his* BROTHER.*)*

SHEPHERD: No wolf. Looked here and there, but no wolf. Found another goat with its neck gone, but no wolf. I don't like it.

DERRICK: *(Writing)* Keep looking.

SHEPHERD: But where? I looked there and here and there and here and nothing. Didn't I, brother?

BROTHER: He did.

SHEPHERD: He comes out at night, is what I think. He sleeps now then doesn't sleep at night. That's what I think. I've never heard him. Just find dead goats. He comes out at night. Stupid to look for him now. Stupid. Isn't it, brother?

BROTHER: Stupid.

SHEPHERD: I'll look again at night 'cause that's when he will come out.

DERRICK: *(Writing)* Do that.

SHEPHERD: I don't have to look more now?

DERRICK: Look tonight.

SHEPHERD: That's a good idea. I'll do that. See the eyes at night, they sparkle. I'll go lie down now, so I can look tonight.... You have visitors. I've seen 'em.

(DERRICK *looks up.*)

SHEPHERD: I saw 'em on the path. Don't like that. They walk stupid. Don't know how to walk on a path, 'cause they're so stupid, is what I think. Shouldn't come here. Is what I think too... One of 'em was here before. Twice before. I remember.

(DERRICK *writes.*)

SHEPHERD: Shouldn't come up here. No. Scare the goats. Scare the sheep. Scare me. I don't like it.

BROTHER: Scare me too.

SHEPHERD: See? See?

(DERRICK *gets up, goes inside.*)

SHEPHERD: What they come up here for?

(BROTHER *shrugs.*)

SHEPHERD: Do I go down there?

(BROTHER *shakes his head.*)

SHEPHERD: Stupid. Is what I think.

(BROTHER *nods.*)

SHEPHERD: I'll kick 'em out. Kick 'em on their pants so they roll back down. I will. I will for sure. Watch... Here they come. Hide! Hide!

(*They run and hide.* POSTMASTER *and two men enter; they are tired from their climb.*)

LAWYER: This it?

POSTMASTER: He raises sheep and goats.

PAUL: Who was that? Somebody just ran back into those trees.

LAWYER: What does one do up here?

POSTMASTER: Raise sheep and goats.

PAUL: Trees. Animals. Quiet. I guess everyone needs to get away. Sometime.

LAWYER: Fifteen years is a bit long for a vacation. His shack?

(POSTMASTER *nods*.)

PAUL: I guess I expected something a little more....

POSTMASTER: A little more what?

PAUL: I don't know. Long fall for a man like Mister Derrick.

LAWYER: Read. Relax. Collect one's thoughts. I've had the urge myself. Though selfishness is not an urge I find worth encouraging.

POSTMASTER: After a couple of visits, I'm convinced he thinks he's found paradise.

PAUL: His paradise. Not mine.

LAWYER: Here he comes. Remember he can't think we are in this for ourselves. He must see the need. As we have.

POSTMASTER: Don't push.

LAWYER: You don't have to push a responsible man, they push themselves.

PAUL: He should jump at the chance. I'd be flattered if I were him.

POSTMASTER: And I'd be satisfied if we just got his signature.

(DERRICK *enters with another piece of paper, he goes to the table, begins to write*.)

POSTMASTER: Hello Hans. *(No response)* Third visit in a week. Hope you don't think me a pest. *(No response)*

Thought you'd like some company. Must get pretty lonely. From time to time. *(No response)* Saw the animals. They're getting fat. Congratulations. Must be a lot of work.

DERRICK: No work getting animals to eat.

POSTMASTER: I guess not. I guess that was a pretty stupid thing to say. Why is it that I always feel stupid talking to you? *(No response)* How's the arm? Did I tell you my arm started to ache? After our last talk? Sympathy pains. That's a joke. The humidity's been awful. Hard to roll out of bed. You ever have that trouble? You lie there thinking about all the things you have to do. Then you sweat. I get this pain in my stomach. Weak stomach. That's what gets me up—it's easier to go do what I have to do than it is to lie there and think about it.... I've thought about what you told me about goat's milk. Fascinating. My wife was a little skeptical. Told her if she'd tasted yours...I promised I'd bring some back....

(Silence; DERRICK writes.)

POSTMASTER: Is this a bad time for you?

DERRICK: For what?

POSTMASTER: I brought some friends.

(DERRICK looks up, then returns to his writing.)

POSTMASTER: They'd like to talk, Hans. *(Pause)* Go ahead.

LAWYER: Mister Derrick...

DERRICK: Who's he?

POSTMASTER: Bill Hamilton. A lawyer, Hans.

DERRICK: He looks like one of my goats. *(Returns to his letter)*

LAWYER: Mister Derrick, the first thing that I think we must make perfectly clear is that we are not in this for our own gain. Not to understand that would be to misinterpret everything we wish to propose. Do you follow me?

POSTMASTER: Don't push.

LAWYER: I am sure that you are aware of the drought, Mister Derrick. Though, I expect, you may not be totally aware of its severity.

PAUL: It's the worst in memory. The chances of any kind of harvest are basically nil. People will starve.

LAWYER: Those who stay.

PAUL: A third of the valley has already left. What businesses remain survive on credit. The entire valley's a bowl for dust.... He's not listening.

POSTMASTER: Keep going.

LAWYER: Simply put, Mister Derrick, we need the works. And these gentlemen and myself are a committee formed for the purpose of convincing you to reclaim the works.

(They look at each other; DERRICK continues to write.)

PAUL: Mister Derrick, Bill here believes that you have an excellent chance with a suit. Given that you built the works and given our present crisis, he thinks certain laws would be bent and what's been boarded up these fifteen years can be unboarded up and given back to you.

LAWYER: All you'd need do, Mister Derrick, is appear at one public meeting, scheduled for this afternoon, and publicly claim what I believe you already own.

PAUL: And we, as a committee, will stand behind you one thousand percent, and will accept responsibility for starting the works up again.

LAWYER: And for running it. Your participation can be as great or as small as you yourself desire. *(Pause)*

PAUL: Mister Derrick?... You have to understand that we, as a committee, could initiate our own legal action.

LAWYER: And in due course I am completely convinced we would succeed in gaining control of the works. But that, Mister Derrick, could take months or even years. A wait that might mean not only the lives of a great number of people, but the life of our valley itself. I don't understand this. I've never been treated like this.

POSTMASTER: Hans, have you heard what we've been saying? Do you understand why we want you to come with us? Do you know what's at stake?! People will starve, don't you care?

PAUL: I don't know what we were thinking of. The man's been up in the hills for fifteen years! Look at him!

LAWYER: If it were his goats starving, he'd care.

POSTMASTER: *(Grabs* DERRICK*)* Hans, if you won't appear, then sign an agreement that'll give us the right to act on your behalf. Bill thinks that might really be all we need. *(Takes out the agreement)* Here. Just your signature... Look at me!!!!

(DERRICK *looks up.*)

POSTMASTER: Keep your goats. Watch the sky. We won't bother you again. But sign. Hans, is that too much to ask?

PAUL: Forget it, he's mad.

POSTMASTER: Madmen have responsibilities too!!! *(Turns back to* DERRICK*)* Sign. We ask only this. Please.

(Long pause. DERRICK *slowly gets up. Looks at all three of them)*

DERRICK: Once a man had a beast inside his breast, his ribs were its cage.

LAWYER: What's he talking about?

POSTMASTER: Sh-sh! Sh-sh!

DERRICK: The beast was mighty and had teeth like a saw and was forever hungry. The man was weak and tired and had not the strength to brush a fly away from his face. All the strength the man had came from his beast, which prowled his chest and growled like a stomach. Everything great this man accomplished in his life was due to the muscle of his beast; and everything terrible was due to this beast as well. One morning the man noticed a dog caught in a rabbit trap clear across the meadow. The man loved dogs and took great pleasure in the way they would curl their necks when they were patted. But the man had not the strength to go and save the dog. So he turns to his beast and says—"beast, give me the strength to pull myself across the meadow." And the beast pushed at the man's ribs and gave him the strength. When the man reached the dog and moved to free it from the trap, the beast stuck out its head from the man's breast and ate the dog. The birds in the treetops watched in horror, but the man shouted— "What did I do? Blame the beast." And the birds replied—but then why didn't you keep the beast locked in your breast? The man sat down and thought and after a half hour he answered— "Without the beast I would not have had the strength to pull myself across the meadow, so can you blame me for wanting to help a wounded dog?" *(Pause)* Well—can you blame him?

(Long pause)

LAWYER: *(To* POSTMASTER*)* What is this?

PAUL: One of his goats would make more sense.

PART THREE

POSTMASTER: Hans??

SHEPHERD: *(From his hiding place)* Growl. Growl. Growl. I'm a wolf. Better run. I'll bite your neck off. Growl! Growl! I'm going to scare you and get your neck! Growl!

LAWYER: What's going on?

PAUL: They're all mad up here.

POSTMASTER: Hans?????

PAUL: Don't waste your breath.

LAWYER: Let's go. I don't like it here. *(Starts to go)*

PAUL: I'm coming.

LAWYER: Hurry. Hurry. Come on.

(They go.)

SHEPHERD: Growl. Growl.

POSTMASTER: I'm sorry. For you. *(He hurries off.)*

SHEPHERD: Growl. Growl. *(He appears.)* How was I? You think they guessed? I think I was a good wolf. Growl. Got them to run off. Scared them. I was going to kick them if I couldn't scare them. But I scared them. Good wolf. Fun. Growl.

(DERRICK folds the letter; puts it in an envelope, hands it to SHEPHERD.)

DERRICK: Here, put this with the rest of them.

SHEPHERD: Another letter to Cockles?

DERRICK: Yes.

(DERRICK goes inside; BROTHER reappears. Pause)

SHEPHERD: Pa always said trouble comes in all colors. First it was the wolf then them. Watch it. Watch out. I didn't like 'em.

(BROTHER shakes his head)

SHEPHERD: So I scare 'em.

(BROTHER *nods.*)

SHEPHERD: Growl. Growl.

BROTHER: Growl.

Scene Three

(GRETCHEN's *garden. Fence. Path. House off right. Chairs. Afternoon*)

(GRETCHEN, *down on her knees, gardening—downstage left.* MEENIE, *with a broom, throwing out a* MAN)

MEENIE: Get out! Out! You've got no business here! I'll stick this through your head! Out! Leave him sleep!!

(MAN *hurries off.* HEINRICH *enters from down the path, from the opposite direction. He stutters.*)

HEINRICH: What was thththat about?

MEENIE: Third one in an hour. Looking to talk to father. Rumors everywhere.

HEINRICH: I heard. Ddddon't know what to think.

MEENIE: I think it's rumors is what I think.

HEINRICH: Lot of people say it's true.

MEENIE: Well I'll believe it when I see it. Let 'em come with their army or whatever they're coming with. Father's going to keep farming like he has.

HEINRICH: People llleaving.

MEENIE: Let 'em.

HEINRICH: Say they're just throwing seed onto rock. Only thing they'll grow is more rrrrrrock. Can't eat rock.

MEENIE: Is that what you say?

PART THREE

HEINRICH: I don't know. No rain. That I do know. Why'd they bring Rip here? Sort of strange.

MEENIE: Closest house. Nothing strange about that.

HEINRICH: Then sort of funny. It beeeeeing Gretchen's house. Is he sick?

MEENIE: Fainted.

HEINRICH: The heat. They fiiight yet?

MEENIE: Who says they'll fight?

HEINRICH: They haven't talked in years. Though when they do talk—and I guess they're going to have to with Rip here—then they'd fiiight.

MEENIE: *(Gestures toward* GRETCHEN*)* Sh-sh.

HEINRICH: She doesn't hear anything when she's gardening. You could scream in her ear and she'd swat you thinking you were a fly. He awake?

MEENIE: The boy?

HEINRICH: Not Nick. Rip. He awake?

MEENIE: Not when I looked in. Neither was Nick, though I better check him what with the noise.

HEINRICH: Meenie…?

MEENIE: What? I'll be right back.

HEINRICH: I wrote a note, Meenie.

MEENIE: No, Heinrich, I don't even want to talk about it.

HEINRICH: Look, if you won't tell your Mother, then let her reeeeead about it. After we're gone.

MEENIE: I haven't said I'm going yet.

HEINRICH: You've said ten times you're going, then when you can't tell your Mother, you change your mind…. I'm going if you're nooooot.

MEENIE: I haven't said I wasn't going either. Just not now.

HEINRICH: When?

MEENIE: Soon. Someday soon. Ohio isn't going to be swallowed up by the earth. It'll still be there when we decide to go.

HEINRICH: I've decided.

MEENIE: Then go!

(Pause)

HEINRICH: And I'm taking Nick with me. After all what's the point in going west, if it's not ffffor your kid.

MEENIE: I got to go check on the boy.

HEINRICH: Boy'll be a man one day. Better to be a man in the west than here. That's all I'm saying. If it were just us, then we could wait. But there's a bbbboy to think about.

MEENIE: You know I can't leave her.

HEINRICH: I know you won't. I don't know why you can't. She's happy. Look at her. She's got her gardening. What she need us for?

MEENIE: It'd kill her.

HEINRICH: But aren't we killing ourselves staying here? And what if the ruuuumors aren't rumors? What if they start up the works? You think they're going to give me a job? People don't forget who you are. The son-in-law of Rip Van Winkle isn't going to be too welcome in those works.

MEENIE: If we take the boy away from her I swear to you she'd die.

HEINRICH: Well how 'bout me?! I'm dying here!

MEENIE: I don't feel like talking about it anymore.

HEINRICH: I'm not asking you to talk about it, I'm sayyyyng, get ourselves packed. I bought a wagon.

(Pause)

MEENIE: You bought a wagon?

HEINRICH: Nice wagon. I gave it a name. I call it "Ohio". One wheel was busted, but I got it fixed. Worked all morning. That's where I've been. Look, Meenie. You know and I know I'm not going without you. And I know I'm going, so that means you're going too. 'Course I wouldn't make you if I thought you didn't want to be made. You've talked about going pretty much as often as I have. Haven't you?!

MEENIE: That was night time talk.

(Long pause)

HEINRICH: Oh. I see. I thought...but never mind.

MEENIE: Heinrich, I didn't mean....

HEINRICH: No. You said what you mean. I didididn't know. That's all.... Then you want me to sell back the wagon? I would, you know.

MEENIE: I know you would, Heinrich. That's why I'm not angry with you cause you bought it, 'cause I know you'd sell it if I asked you.

HEINRICH: You asking me?

(Pause)

MEENIE: I'll go see the boy.

HEINRICH: I said, are you asking me?

MEENIE: I haven't said anything.

HEINRICH: No?

MEENIE: No... Give me your note.

HEINRICH: You want it?

MEENIE: I want to read it. I haven't said anything.

HEINRICH: No... Should I go pack some goods in the wagon in case you do say something?

MEENIE: You want to go today?!!

HEINRICH: We have the wagon.

MEENIE: I might change my mind. I might.

HEINRICH: *I know.*

MEENIE: As long as you know—then go ahead.

(Pause. HEINRICH *looks at* MEENIE, *smiles then hurries off. She starts to go inside, reading the note. She stops, turns to* GRETCHEN, *goes to her and hugs her. Then runs inside.* GRETCHEN *looks up.* PAUL *enters from the path. He looks around.)*

PAUL: *(To* GRETCHEN*)* Excuse me, I understand Mister Van Winkle was brought here. Could you tell me if he's awake?

(RIP *appears from the house.)*

RIP: What do you want?

PAUL: Don't be hostile, Rip. No one sent me. I came to help.

RIP: Offer me no help. Help yourself. Get out. *(Turns away)*

PAUL: There's talk, Rip.

RIP: The Lord says: whether he be friend or foe, talk not of other's lives. Goodbye.

PAUL: He also says something about heeding warnings. What I've heard, I think you ought to listen to.

RIP: My daughter's inside. She's already thrown three of you out. Strong girl. I watched from the window. She can use a broom like you or I can use a fork, I'll call her.

PAUL: One minute is all, Rip. I'm not in this for myself. It's for the valley.

RIP: The biggest thief's the first to deny he is one. He doesn't even wait to be asked.

PAUL: And the biggest fool is the one who hears what the blind see. There is a drought. Do you understand? Do you care? Starving people aren't plants that will sprout again in the spring.

RIP: Affliction does not come from the dust, nor does trouble sprout from the ground; but man is born to trouble as the sparks fly upward. So says the Lord. *(Turns)*

PAUL: You're a fool. I'll take the abuse and your pompous attitude. But I'll be the first in line to see your face when Derrick arrives.

RIP: Derrick?

PAUL: Suddenly an interest? Like magic. I've found the magical name.

RIP: What do you mean—Derrick?

PAUL: There's talk, that he's come to reclaim his works.

RIP: He has no works.

PAUL: Not as yet.

RIP: What he had he'd stolen.

PAUL: True.

RIP: Anyway, he raises goats in the hills.

PAUL: Did. Some of your friends—your farmer friends—have been calling on Derrick. It appears they have little faith in a harvest. A works would mean jobs.

RIP: I don't believe it.

PAUL: The flesh is weak, Rip.

RIP: A rumor.

PAUL: Which everyone now believes. There's a petition going around which demands that you turn over the works.

RIP: To Derrick?

PAUL: To a committee of businessmen.

RIP: Who's on this committee?

PAUL: I don't know. It's been kept secret.

RIP: And the committee will turn over the works to Derrick, when he arrives?

PAUL: That hasn't been decided yet.... A third of the valley has already left.

RIP: Not to join Derrick.

PAUL: That is the talk, Rip.

(Pause; RIP *obviously upset)*

RIP: *(More to himself)* I don't understand. How can they turn? We have moved this earth like it was our own muscle. We've flexed the ground, thumbed in the seeds, sweated a rain, nursed the stalk, slapped the harvest 'til it cried. It's been my body. It's been me. *(Short pause)* No. I will not sell it, barter it, share it, or give it away. We've had harvests that would choke a horn of plenty. How can they run? We are farmers. We plow the land, furrow the brow of the earth and make it think it's richer than it is. When the ground breathes, it's because we are its lungs! No! I don't understand. No. They can't take it away! No!!!! Not now, not tomorrow—never!!!!!

(Pause)

PAUL: Are you going to tear down the works?

RIP: Why would I do that?

PAUL: There'd be nothing to take from you then.

RIP: I don't know. Why rip down something that you've forgotten about?

PAUL: But you might? Because others haven't forgotten?

RIP: I said, I don't know. Now get out. Go away. But if you find out who's on this committee, I'd pay to know. Go. Go.

(PAUL *leaves.*)

RIP: Cowards. Thieves. Gutless dogs. They get a sliver in their finger and they scream like they are dying. Their faith's as tangible as a hot breeze. If they can't plow a field with the toe of their boot, then they cry and whine that the ground's too hard, and they give up and whip up the dust as they flee, instead of whipping themselves to keep at their work. They'd rather eat promises of better things to come than drink that sweat off their lips which comes from making things better.... There must be a million wrinkles on God's Face, each one lining His disappointment in us. (*Pause*)

GRETCHEN: I'm afraid I've given Him a wrinkle or two myself.

(RIP *turns to* GRETCHEN.)

GRETCHEN: Hello. I heard. I'm sorry.

RIP: What are you sorry for? Derrick's coming. You'll have him back in your bed.

(GRETCHEN *turns away.*)

RIP: Forgive me. I didn't mean it.... Not a very tactful way to begin a conversation after fifteen years. How are you?

(GRETCHEN *nods.*)

RIP: I am sorry. I know you left Derrick. His coming will be as hard on you as it will on me.... That was stupid. Thank you for putting me up.

GRETCHEN: No one asked me.

RIP: And if they had? *(Silence)* I'd better go. *(Starts to go, stops)* Hot. I'd never fainted before. Meenie's been after me to drop by for years. I used to say I'd have to be dragged. I guess I almost was. What are you planting? Peas?

GRETCHEN: Flowers.

RIP: Can't eat flowers.

GRETCHEN: That's why I grow them.

(Long pause)

RIP: I'll go.... What will you do? If he comes, I mean.

GRETCHEN: Why should I do anything?

RIP: I just thought that.... It's not important. I suspect he'll have the works to occupy himself.

GRETCHEN: Then you'll let him take it?

RIP: If it's God's will.

GRETCHEN: Is it?

RIP: I'll pray. Then I'll see *(Pause)*

GRETCHEN: I have my garden.

RIP: Yes. It'll be lovely.

GRETCHEN: And there's Meenie. And Heinrich.

RIP: Yes.

GRETCHEN: And the boy. Between him and the garden I have my hands full.

RIP: I peeked in on him a moment ago. Handsome child. The way children sleep—I'd like to sleep like that again. Meenie's brought him over a couple of times. I've found I enjoy playing Grandfather. I think I'm a good horse—or my knee is. She's hinted that you didn't know, but I always assumed that you did. *(Pause)* What kind of flowers?

GRETCHEN: Roses.

RIP: From seeds? But that'll take years.

(GRETCHEN *turns away. Pause*)

RIP: Right. What's the.…. What is the hurry? Why do I feel like an idiot right now? *(Long pause)* Have you ever tried to hold onto a rope as it was being pulled through your fingers? You concentrate on every inch, and every inch as it's pulled through seems at the time like a tremendous loss. A catastrophe. Then as feet and yards pass through your clenched hands, a panic almost sets in. Your heart pounds faster. Your breathing gets quicker. It's a very desperate feeling. But it's desperate only because you think that at any moment the end of the rope will pass through your fingers. It could come in five minutes. Tomorrow. Next year. If only you could convince yourself that the rope had no end, then there would be no reason to panic. You could still struggle 'til your muscles broke, the effort needn't be any less. Without an end, without something to struggle for or to struggle to prevent, that I believe would be a wonderful way to live. Then I think I could say to myself, "what is the hurry?" and be convinced. *(Silence)* I'm babbling. I don't know why I'm talking like this. *(Long pause. He turns to leave.)*

GRETCHEN: Because I didn't interrupt you…because I'm your wife.

(Pause)

RIP: My…? What?

GRETCHEN: Sh-sh. Let us just keep that one thought simple. If we can. *(She gets up to leave.)*

RIP: Gretchen…?

GRETCHEN: Do we have to suffer over everything?

RIP: But…

GRETCHEN: Don't ask.

(Pause)

RIP: Gretchen...I didn't know.

GRETCHEN: Neither did I, Rip. *(She turns to go inside.)*

RIP: But why didn't you...?

GRETCHEN: Don't ask! *(Pause)* I guess I've been wanting to see you. Because when they brought you here this morning and I thought you'd died, I heard myself think—my luck, when he comes he's dead. Then when they told me you'd fainted in the heat, I almost ran away. Don't ask me why, Rip. *(Turns again to go inside)*

RIP: I don't understand. *(Short pause)* I would have come, but you didn't ask.

(Pause)

GRETCHEN: I'd have asked, but you wouldn't have come.

(Pause. Noise of a crowd off. HEINRICH *enters.)*

GRETCHEN: Heinrich, what's going on?

HEINRICH: The inn. Must be most of the town outside the inn. There's a meeting.

GRETCHEN: Maybe Derrick's come.

*(*RIP *just looks at* GRETCHEN.*)*

GRETCHEN: You'd better go, Rip. *(Short pause)* Go.

RIP: Gretchen...

GRETCHEN: Hurry. Hurry.

*(*RIP *hesitates.* GRETCHEN *goes inside.* RIP *hurries off.* MEENIE *comes out with a pile of laundry.)*

HEINRICH: The supplies are in the wagon.

MEENIE: How'd you do it so fast?

HEINRICH: I didididid it this morning.

MEENIE: Heinrich...

HEINRICH: You've changed your mind. *(He turns to leave.)*

MEENIE: The letter, Heinrich.

HEINRICH: Yes?

MEENIE: It's on her dresser.

Scene Four

(An Inn. Table. Three chairs. Door to the street POSTMASTER stands in the doorway, looking out. LAWYER and PAUL sit behind the table listening to the noise of the large angry crowd outside. Pause)

POSTMASTER: They've picked three to do their talking.

LAWYER: Show them in.

(POSTMASTER goes out, closing the door behind him. Crowd noise becomes distant.)

PAUL: What are we going to tell them?

LAWYER: The truth. Of course.

PAUL: Of course. I'll get some chairs.

(Goes Off. Door opens. Noise again, loud. FIRST FARMER, SECOND FARMER, and DUTCH enter with the POSTMASTER. They close the door. Noise becomes distant again. Long pause)

LAWYER: Hello, Sam. How's the missus?

FIRST FARMER: Hungry

LAWYER: She's a good woman.

FIRST FARMER: Not when she don't eat.

(Short pause. PAUL enters with chairs.)

LAWYER: Sit.

SECOND FARMER: Where's Rip? It's him we wanted to talk to.

LAWYER: We didn't feel that was necessary.

SECOND FARMER: Then it's true, what everybody's sayin'.

LAWYER: Sit.

(Short pause. The FARMERS sit.)

LAWYER: *(To* PAUL*)* Should I start?

(PAUL *nods.)*

LAWYER: Gentlemen, believe me when I say that we can appreciate your anxieties. And it is with the hope of relieving some of them that we have called this meeting this afternoon.

DUTCH: You ain't called nothing, it just happened.

FIRST FARMER: Let the man talk, Dutch.

DUTCH: You don't eat talk.

FIRST FARMER: Go 'head.

LAWYER: Gentlemen, a great number of rumors have gripped our town....

DUTCH: What does he mean "rumors"?!

LAWYER: I repeat—rumors have gripped our town these past few weeks, and some of us have felt the need to form a committee whose purpose would be to dispel such rumors as best we can. But before we go on, let me just add that we are all aware of the crisis our valley is going through. And after what we've been up against, one begins to wonder if plague and pestilence are to be next.

(LAWYER *smiles and chuckles.* PAUL *chuckles as well. The* FARMERS *just stare at him.)*

LAWYER: Yes. I think we should all be quite proud of ourselves, our response and resilience has been admirable.

SECOND FARMER: We don't need to hear no speech. You just tell us how you're planning to stop Rip.

LAWYER: Please, let me just finish by saying....

DUTCH: More talk.

LAWYER: ...by saying how proud we are of each and every one of you and how pleased to know you all as friends.

DUTCH: There are friends and there are friends.

FIRST FARMER: Just tell us Mister Hamilton. And tell us simple. What are you going to do about stoppin' Rip?

PAUL: Stopping him from what, Sam?

SECOND FARMER: Where you been? He's raisin' an army. *(To* FIRST FARMER:*)* If he don't even know that I don't know why we're talkin' to them, Sam.

LAWYER: Paul...?

PAUL: Gentlemen, Mister Van Winkle has no intention of raising an army.

SECOND FARMER: See, he knows nothin'. We're wasting our time, we should be talkin' to Rip.

FIRST FARMER: Mister Hamilton, Dutch has seen some letters.

DUTCH: I didn't say I really saw them, Sam.

FIRST FARMER: Dutch, you told me you saw letters.

PAUL: I think our postmaster would know if any such letters went out. Have there been?

POSTMASTER: *(Standing by the door)* No.

(Pause)

SECOND FARMER: If there's no army, then who's gonna fight Derrick? Us? Like hell we will.

LAWYER: Mister Derrick has raised no army. Is raising no army. And has no plans to raise an army.

SECOND FARMER: I don't believe that.

LAWYER: We visited with him only this afternoon.

SECOND FARMER: Today?

PAUL: We felt compelled to find the truth.

LAWYER: And though I will admit Mister Derrick showed some curiosity in our situation, I'd have to say, his interest was rather minimal. Wouldn't you agree, Paul?

PAUL: Definitely.

SECOND FARMER: So he's not coming?

(LAWYER *shakes his head.*)

FIRST FARMER: Wait. Then he's buying the works. That's what he's doing. Somebody told me that and I didn't believe him.

LAWYER: Sam, I can say categorically, that no sale of the works has ever been proposed and no potential buyer has ever been approached by Van Winkle or by anyone acting in his behalf.

SECOND FARMER: He's not sellin', Sam.

DUTCH: What about the wagon he bought? Where's he running off to with a wagon?

LAWYER: Paul, you can answer that better than I can.

PAUL: I'm the one who sold the wagon. Though not to Rip, but to his son-in-law, Heinrich. I'm sure you know that Heinrich's been talking for quite some time now about moving to Ohio. I guess he finally decided to stop talking and do it.

PART THREE

POSTMASTER: Or he finally got his wife to go with him!

(The FARMERS turn to the POSTMASTER and smile and chuckle.)

SECOND FARMER: How'd he get her to do that? I'd like to know his secret.

DUTCH: Wish he could persuade my wife to go with him. *(Laughs)*

FIRST FARMER: Need a bigger wagon than that for your wife.

SECOND FARMER: He could tie her to the back and let her roll. *(Laughs)*

LAWYER: Gentlemen, if that's everything... *(Stands)*

FIRST FARMER: *(Looks at the other two FARMERS)* I guess it is.

DUTCH: What are we going to tell 'em?

FIRST FARMER: Go home. Gotta rain sometime.

(They start to leave.)

PAUL: Just one second.

(They stop and turn.)

PAUL: I feel sort of foolish bringing this up.

LAWYER: Go ahead, Paul.

PAUL: And please don't misunderstand me. It is only in this spirit of wiping the slate completely clean that I even talk about this. And please, I am not suggesting that this be the case, it's only something I've heard. But in all fairness to Rip, I feel we must clear the air.

DUTCH: What are you talking about? What've you heard?

PAUL: Please understand how much I admire Rip, and to me at least such an action would be completely out of his character.

POSTMASTER: Paul, maybe this could wait.

SECOND FARMER: No, let him talk.

PAUL: So with all this in mind, I visited Rip just a half hour ago and asked him to his face to either confirm or deny.

POSTMASTER: Confirm or deny what?

PAUL: And all I can say is that he did not deny it.

DUTCH: Deny what?!!

PAUL: That he was going to tear down the works.

FIRST FARMER: He's going to tear down the works?

SECOND FARMER: Why would he do that?

PAUL: I don't know. *(Pause)*

DUTCH: It's true. Damn it, it's true!!!!

SECOND FARMER: What is?

THIRD FARMER: Everything!!!!

(He goes to the door and flings it open. Loud crowd noise)

POSTMASTER: Gentlemen, please! I'm sure there's an explanation!

(The FARMER stop at the doorway, look out. The crowd slowly gets quiet. Silence. RIP enters, having walked through the crowds.)

RIP: I'm confused. What's going on here? I don't believe what I've just heard out there.... Sam, your boy just threw a rock at me.

(SAM turns away.)

RIP: I don't understand. *(To FIRST FARMER:)* Close the door.

(Hesitates, and then does)

RIP: Why aren't you in the fields? There's work to be done.

(Short pause)

LAWYER: Rip...

RIP: I'm not talking to you! *(Looks at the* FARMERS*)* We are friends. And 'til now that was the source of tremendous pride for me. We have worked together. And whereas no single man grows a crop, each one of us shares in its glory. Dutch, what did they mean by calling me a traitor?

(Short pause. DUTCH *starts to leave,* RIP *grabs him.)*

RIP: What is happening here?!!!! *(Short pause)* When I first took over the fields, fifteen years ago, my urge was not to build a mecca of wonder. I wanted no Babylon. My urge was more conservative—I envisioned a simple valley, a valley where one lives at peace and hard work; one where neighbors care for each other, share with each other, live for each other. Where one's tasks were simply defined and where all that separated one from a successful completion of one's task was hard laborious work. I know things have been hard, but work is still the heart beat of this valley, without it, it will die. I believe in nothing, if I do not believe in hard work. Fantasy and dreams have no home in the breast of a hard working man. And when one fails, failure is not measured by the lack of the growth of a crop, or by the absence of rain, it is measured only be the lack of faith in one's ability to work!

*(*SECOND FARMER *moves away.)*

RIP: Please. Listen. Our valley is young. There shall be droughts again. There shall be storms that will drown the tops of corn stalks. There shall be disease and death and hatred and sin. And this shall be as we, our valley, grow old. As a boat in a storm we can't abandon ship, but must weather the winds and the rocks and the tides of the moon, we must work our masts, scoop the seawater out of our hulls, we must work until our hands are stubs. This work may not save our harvest, but it will show what kind of men we are. Look for hope only here! *(Raises his hand)* Hope is a calloused hand! *(Short pause)* It is easy to complain, it is hard to work hard. God gave us sleep as our reward for work. If we do not sleep well, if we wake up tearful, lamenting, and complaining, it is only because we have not worked hard enough. *(Pause)* Try to run to a greener valley, but where do you run when it too has a drought? We could rebuild a works and hire ourselves as laborers and depend upon other valleys to buy what we make. But as farmers, we can depend upon ourselves. We need no one else. We need but two hands, a neck that aches, legs that crumble from tiredness, and there in our fields, stooped and ready to die, we will have breathed our last breath out of exhaustion and we will know then what it means to work as only men can. And only then shall we die men. God put us here on earth not to dream, not to hope, not to run away and hide, but to sweat and to die…. That is our purpose. *(Pause)* Come, there's work to be—

(Suddenly DUTCH *takes his hoe and smashes it on the table.)*

RIP: Wait. Wait. Wrong!

(FARMERS *open the door. Loud, angry crowd grows.)*

Scene Five (a)

(A street. GRETCHEN *enters with the letter. She cries.)*

GRETCHEN: Oh God! Oh God! Meenie!!!! Meenie!!!!

(Sobs. RIP *hobbles in; his face is cut.)*

RIP: There you are. Where's Meenie and the boy? We've got to go. It's madness. They would have killed me. Friends. They call themselves friends. Come on, if

PART THREE

we can make it across the hills, we can sit and wait this thing out. I've never seen anything like it. The whole town's spooked. Get up! Get up! What's the matter with you?

GRETCHEN: Look. *(Hands him the letter)*

RIP: Thank God, they must have known. Hurry. Hurry. *(Tries to pull her)*

GRETCHEN: Why didn't they tell me?!! Why'd they have to leave a letter?!!!

RIP: It's the best thing they could have done, Gretchen.

GRETCHEN: I want to see the boy!!!!!

RIP: Come on, if we move fast enough maybe we can catch them as they come through the pass. It's quicker over the hills.

GRETCHEN: Catch them?

RIP: Or just follow 'em to Ohio. I don't know, Gretchen, we can't stay here!!

GRETCHEN: You'll come with me?

RIP: Of course, I'm coming. What do you think I've been saying? I'm not going to stay put and be crucified. Come on, we'll need some sacks from your house. They'll be on their way to my house by now. Expect to see it burning by the time we reach the woods.

GRETCHEN: What's happened? What's happened?

RIP: Come with me.

(GRETCHEN *suddenly stops. Looks at* RIP)

GRETCHEN: With you? *(Pause)*

RIP: We'll catch 'em. *(Pause)*

GRETCHEN: Look at your face.

RIP: I've seen the devil. Hurry. Hurry.

(GRETCHEN *and* RIP *go.*)

Scene Five (b)

(The same. Half hour later. LAWYER *and* PAUL, *standing together. Down the road come two* FARMERS.*)*

PAUL: Gone.

LAWYER: Better for us. Could have been messy.

FIRST FARMER: *(To* SECOND FARMER:*)* Half way to New York by now.

SECOND FARMER: We should have known, what with him buying a wagon.

FIRST FARMER: He must think we're real stupid.

SECOND FARMER: Not stupid, just weak. Hurry. We might still catch him.

(They run out.)

POSTMASTER: *(Entering)* Gone?

*(*PAUL *nods.)*

PAUL: Would have been easier if he'd just stepped aside on his own. But at least it's done.

POSTMASTER: Better this way—clean break. New beginning. They're ransacking his house.

LAWYER: As long as it's just his house.

POSTMASTER: Poor Rip. What if they catch up with him?

LAWYER: He's got a good head start.

PAUL: Watch that "poor Rip" talk. Don't want a backlash. Folks can turn sentimental as fast as they can turn angry.

LAWYER: We'll have to keep our fingers in the air, seeing how the wind blows.

POSTMASTER: And if it starts blowing at us?

LAWYER: We'll turn and blow with 'em. We could always name the works after him.

PAUL: After who?

LAWYER: After Rip. The Van Winkle Works. If they start getting nervous about what they've done, that should soothe their throbbing consciences.

POSTMASTER: The Van Winkle Works. I like that.

PAUL: Could have a little ceremony. Once things get calmer.

POSTMASTER: It's the least we could do.

LAWYER: The least.

POSTMASTER: Bring the valley together. A fresh start. It's for the good of the valley.

PAUL: And what's the good for the valley, is good for everyone.

LAWYER: Come. Let's go and get down to work.

(They leave.)

Scene Six (a)

(The hills. Evening. Wind. DERRICK *enters.)*

DERRICK: *(Calling)* Ho! Ho! Shepherd, ho! *(To himself:)* I've watched one hundred ants race in circles and dance in lines. They know what's coming. They know what's coming. I've witnessed the sky, with white puffs billowing and dark puffs born from underneath. From these two observations, I know it will rain. Between the lowly ants of the earth and the high clouds of the sky, one needs nothing in between. *(Calls)* Ho! Ho! *(To himself:)* Time tells itself one need not ask a man for the time.

*(*SHEPHERD *runs in.)*

SHEPHERD: I'm here. I'm here. Though I've left my breath back there.

DERRICK: Then it'll be washed away. I've been calling.

SHEPHERD: And I've been running.

DERRICK: And I've been looking.

SHEPHERD: And I've been running.

DERRICK: And I've been waiting.

SHEPHERD: And I've been running.

DERRICK: Then your feet are as slow as your mind. Look at the sky.

SHEPHERD: Ah.

DERRICK: It's going to rain.

SHEPHERD: Yes.

DERRICK: And there'll be wind.

SHEPHERD: Yes.

DERRICK: And lightning and blasts of thunder.

SHEPHERD: Yes, that too.

DERRICK: So?

SHEPHERD: So?

DERRICK: Are you a shepherd or not?

SHEPHERD: I am a shepherd. Yes, I am a shepherd.

DERRICK: Then are you a good shepherd?

SHEPHERD: A good shepherd? Let me think. What's a good shepherd?

DERRICK: One who knows that sheep and goats run off when it thunders.

SHEPHERD: Oh, I know that. Then I'm a good shepherd.

DERRICK: Then you know that a good shepherd gathers his flock together when it thunders.

SHEPHERD: Oh, I know that too.

DERRICK: Then do it.

PART THREE

SHEPHERD: Done.

DERRICK: What do you mean—done? That's why I've been calling you, to tell you what to do.

SHEPHERD: And that's why I've been running, gathering up the goats. One doesn't have to watch the sky to know it will pour tonight.

DERRICK: No?

SHEPHERD: It always pours tonight. Because of the spirits. Tonight is the night. Even the stupidest men know that. My brother knows that.

DERRICK: You know that there are spirits?

SHEPHERD: I know what I know. And that tonight is the night. Every fifteen years the spirits of a man called Hudson and his crew, they light the sky and crack the ears.

DERRICK: How is that?

SHEPHERD: They light their pipes and play tenpins. Tonight's the night. I know.

DERRICK: You head has sweat your brains, shepherd. And I suppose tonight your wolf becomes a prince?

SHEPHERD: A prince? Why would a wolf become a prince? That only happens in fairy stories. I am no child. I don't believe in fairy stories. No. The wolf is still a wolf. And that's next. I will now look for the wolf, but had to gather the goats first. Then the wolf. I'll wait and watch for him. And the spirits.

DERRICK: You might as well look to yourself for a thought as look for spirits

SHEPHERD: No, they are here. I've seen 'em.

DERRICK: Seen what?

SHEPHERD: Two spirits. One an old man and one a woman, that's the shape they've taken for tonight.

DERRICK: What did you say to these spirits?

SHEPHERD: I only watched. I'm scared to talk to spirits.

DERRICK: Then how do you know they're spirits, shepherd?

SHEPHERD: Because they're here tonight! But if you want, I can prove it to you, though proving spirits is like proving the sun will shine. It just is.

DERRICK: How can you prove they are spirits.

SHEPHERD: They don't bleed. It's like knifing smoke or water to knife a spirit. They don't cry out. That is how you prove. I go. I go. (*Runs off*)

DERRICK: Shepherd, wait!... Ah, let him go chase the shadows of trees, that is all that's up here tonight. (*Long pause*) Wind. Blow. (*Pause*) It will rain. And make everything soft. Like a sponge. Or a face. (*He goes.*)

Scene Six (b)

(*The hills. Evening.* GRETCHEN *and* RIP *enter.*)

GRETCHEN: Rip, are you crying?

RIP: I'm hating. I can't keep the hate down my throat. Every time I take a deep breath it claws its way up my neck. I shouldn't have looked back. Maybe we should sit and rest.

GRETCHEN: Why? I can walk. I can walk.

RIP: Your eyes keep closing. (*He falls.*) Ahhh!

GRETCHEN: What happened?

RIP: I stepped in a hole.

GRETCHEN: Give me your hand.

(RIP *turns.*)

GRETCHEN: What is it?

PART THREE

RIP: I thought I heard someone. *(Listens)* No.

GRETCHEN: Who would be up here? You don't think they're following you?

RIP: "The Lord is my shepherd; I shall not want.
He maketh me to lie down in green pastures.
He leadeth me beside the still waters; He restoreth my soul.
He leadeth me in the paths of righteousness for His name's sake.
Yea, though I walk through the valley of the shadow of death,
I will fear no evil: for thou art with me:
Thy rod and they staff they comfort me."
(He looks up.) Look. Up there. Past the moon. Clouds. When's the last time we've seen clouds?

GRETCHEN: Could be a night mist. Sh-sh! Listen!

(Distant howl)

GRETCHEN: There. Let's go.

RIP: I think we should rest.

GRETCHEN: We'll have the rest of our lives to rest once we catch up with them. Come on.

RIP: I want to sit for a minute.

GRETCHEN: I'll walk on ahead. You can catch up.

RIP: No. Stay with me. Sit.

(GRETCHEN *does.*)

RIP: Put your head on my lap. I'd like that.

(GRETCHEN *does.*)

RIP: Comfortable? Any rocks?

(GRETCHEN *shakes her head.*)

RIP: Let me get the hair out of your eyes. *(Short pause)* The dark is nice. I like it best like this. With all the blackness you can still dream of light. But in the day, with all the light, all you see is black.

(GRETCHEN *has fallen asleep.*)

RIP: I've forgotten how much a sleeping woman looks like an angel.

(SHEPHERD *enters.*)

RIP: Who's there?! Who's there?!

SHEPHERD: Oh. Oh. The spirit's seen me. Hide. Hide. *(Runs off)*

RIP: *(Whispers)* Hello? Hello? *(Short pause)* The wind's really come up.

(Pause; thunder)

RIP: What?

(Thunder)

RIP: Again! Gretchen. *(Shakes her)* Gretchen!!!!!

GRETCHEN: What? What is it?

RIP: Listen!!!!!

GRETCHEN: To what? I don't hear anything. The wagon? You heard the wagon?!

RIP: No. No. Sh-sh. Listen. *(Thunder)* Hear it? Hear it? *(Thunder)*

GRETCHEN: Thunder?

RIP: Yes.

GRETCHEN: Thunder.

RIP: Yes!

GRETCHEN: It's not the wagon. It's thunder.

RIP: Gretchen, it's going to rain.

GRETCHEN: Is it?

(Short pause)

PART THREE

RIP: Listen... Hear it?

GRETCHEN: Do you know if they bought a covered wagon?

RIP: It's raining, Gretchen.

GRETCHEN: Maybe we should find some cover. We'll get wet.

RIP: Some cover? Gretchen we don't have to look for cover. It's raining!

GRETCHEN: Yes.

RIP: Don't you know what that means?

GRETCHEN: We'll get wet.

RIP: Get up. Come on, get up. It's raining!!! *(Laughs)* Dear God— "I have heard of thee by the hearing of the ear, but now my eyes see Thee!" Hurry, we can be back by dawn. Gretchen, feel it! Rain!!!!

GRETCHEN: So?

RIP: We'll let them see who has not flinched, who has not wavered, but has stood the ground. Let this be their lesson and let them be the better for it. We'll plow and plant by the moon if we have to. But there will be a harvest!! Get up. Hurry. Let's go.

GRETCHEN: I'm not going.

RIP: What do you mean, you're not going? It's raining. Feel it. It rains!!!

GRETCHEN: I'm not going.

RIP: What's the matter with you? Don't you understand? The drought's over, Gretchen. There will be no reason to start up the works. Because it rains!!! We have struggled and suffered and God has said— enough. Enough. There's no reason anymore to keep running.

GRETCHEN: There is for me. Rain or no rain.

RIP: Look, we'll call back Meenie. I'll send a wagon. Ten wagons! They'll come back.

GRETCHEN: I'm not going, Rip.

(Long pause. RIP *backs away from* GRETCHEN.*)*

RIP: *(Suddenly screams)* Gretchen, don't destroy this for me!!!!!!!

GRETCHEN: I don't wish to destroy anything.

RIP: My life and work's down there. God in His great compassion has given me it all back. I can't deny Him!!!!

GRETCHEN: Then go.

RIP: They'll come back!

GRETCHEN: Leave me.

RIP: Don't be stupid. I can't leave you up here.

GRETCHEN: Go. Go.

RIP: Do you hate me so much?!

GRETCHEN: *(Screams:)* No!!!!!!!!!!!!!

RIP: I don't understand how you can do this to me!!!

GRETCHEN: *(Crying)* I'm not doing anything to you!

RIP: Has nothing changed? From the beginning, you've done your best to keep me crawling. Keep me on my knees and begging!!!! *(Erupts)* What did Derrick do, pay you to keep me up here so the two of you can steal my land again?!!!!

GRETCHEN: That's not fair, Rip. Meenie!!!! She's all I have.

RIP: Maybe I'm her father and maybe I'm not.

GRETCHEN: How can you!!!! Leave me!!!!

RIP: It'd serve you right if I did.

GRETCHEN: I've been alone up here before!

PART THREE

RIP: Doing what? Whoring with Derrick?!!!!!!!

(GRETCHEN *slaps* RIP.)

RIP: Still scratching like a rabid dog. (*Short pause. He hits her.*)

(GRETCHEN *screams.*)

GRETCHEN: I was up here looking for you!

RIP: What?

GRETCHEN: For you!!!!!

RIP: Right. Don't weight your soul with any more lies, or it'll be so heavy it won't be able to fly a foot!

GRETCHEN: (*Sobbing*) For five years I looked. I'm up here every day. Every day. First, I'm looking for the body of my husband. Then just the bones. Until mad or half-crazed, I don't know, and one day my legs seem to break and my head, it goes dark and I wake up months later in a bed.

RIP: I don't know what you're talking about!

GRETCHEN: And while I was ill, they told me later how they'd dug my grave. And Derrick, he's taken Meenie as a ward, and so still in bed, I married him, because of being so kind.

RIP: Have you no shame? Why do I want to hear this?

GRETCHEN: No!!!! You have to listen!!!!! All the time I'm married to Derrick, I don't know what that paper said that he wanted you to sign. I think it's just what they'd told me—a promise to stay sober.

RIP: You're lying. You knew! You knew!!!

GRETCHEN: I knew when you came back, and so I leave Derrick, because I hate him. I leave him not because he lost the works, but because I hate him!!!! And I hate me, for marrying the man who wished to destroy my husband.

(RIP *turns away.*)

GRETCHEN: Wait!!!! Listen!!!

(RIP *turns back.*)

GRETCHEN: And since you've come back, I've done all I could do to do my duty, and be your wife.

RIP: Gretchen, please.

GRETCHEN: I've tried to be a good wife, Rip. God knows how I've tried; He knows how many years I've been sending Meenie to see you.

RIP: You? ...I don't understand.

GRETCHEN: No. I not only knew, but I sent her. I wanted you to see your child. Watch her grow. Be her father. And I used her visits to learn about you—I know what you eat. How you dress. In my mind, I've nursed you when you've been sick. I've watched you for hours through her words; and heard your voice speak in her mouth.

RIP: No. No. Gretchen...?

GRETCHEN: No. Don't say anything! ...Haven't you ever noticed flowers on your table? Shirts in your dresser that have been washed? A polished floor? Hot bread in your kitchen and wondered how did this all happen?

RIP: I thought Meenie....

GRETCHEN: It happened while you were in the field and I've come into your home and worked like a wife in the only way I could. I was determined to be your wife, Rip, though without ever seeing you until today.

RIP: I don't understand. Why didn't Meenie ever tell me?

GRETCHEN: Because I wouldn't let her. I was afraid then I'd have to see you. It seemed better like this.

PART THREE

RIP: Then come with me now. Be my wife.

GRETCHEN: *(Crying)* No.

RIP: *(Erupts)* Why not?!!!!!

GRETCHEN: I've lived without you and can again, but the thought of life without Meenie and her boy, is a thought I couldn't live. Go. Leave me! Please, Rip. I've hurt you, don't let me hurt you more. Meenie and the boy are all I have; they're what I am. I have not hurt them—yet. Go. I won't ask you to come with me, because I understand: it rains, it rains. Go. Go... Bye. *(She hurries off.)*

RIP: Gretchen! Gretchen!

(RIP hesitates looks up at the rain. Thunder and lightning)

RIP: Gretchen, wait!!!! ...Wait!!!! ...Stop, Stop!!!!!!!

(Thunder and lightning. He starts to go in her direction. The SHEPHERD hurries in and stabs RIP in the back. RIP groans and falls. Thunder and lightning)

SHEPHERD: *(Looks at his knife)* Blood. Blood. Must be only part spirit. Because he groans too. Yes, he groans. But does he hurt? I think no, 'cause spirits don't hurt. I better tell Derrick that I have caught us a spirit. And a spirit's even better than a wolf. Ho! Ho!

(Runs out. Storm. DERRICK enters.)

DERRICK: Shepherd! Shepherd! With this thunder I've seen two goats already run from the herd. And if this rain keeps up this will be a hill of mud and it'll be hell to unstuck them. Shepherd! *(Sees RIP)* What's this? A man. A curious place for a man in a rainstorm. In a rain a tree can sprout new limbs, though I think a man should not have such hopes. Hello? Hello? Are you asleep? ...He doesn't answer. He may be asleep or maybe not. Hello? Are you dead?

(RIP groans.)

DERRICK: He groans so he's not dead. I'll get closer. *(Looks at* RIP. *Long pause)* This face. I think I know it. *(Short pause)* And if there's one thing I know it's that I know faces. I see them all the time. When I close my eyes I see them too. I think this is one that I have seen with my eyes closed. *(Pause. Looks at* RIP:*)* Wait. He's saying something….

RIP: Gretchen…

DERRICK: Gretchen? He says "Gretchen". Now there's a name I know very well. My answer's yes. Yes. If the question is if I have heard of a Gretchen. It is yes. Wait. He's speaking again

RIP: Gretchen. Gretchen.

DERRICK: Oh. Gretchen Gretchen. Now that is a name I do not know. I once knew a Benjamin Benjamin, but I have never known a Gretchen Gretchen. I am sorry. But come, this is no place to get acquainted. Let's get out of this rain before the mud rises like a tide…. I know your face…and we both know a Gretchen, though you know both a Gretchen and a Gretchen Gretchen. But still we have much in common. Come, I'll sit you down in a chair and talk to you and if you die I'll keep the bugs off you `til you rot. Come. Come. You look sleepy. Here put this on. *(Puts his coat on him)* It rains. Come.

(DERRICK *carries* RIP *off.*)

Scene Six (c)

(The hills. Rain. Wind. SHEPHERD *runs in.)*

SHEPHERD: Ahh! Ahh! Oh Lord, I have been looking for Derrick, but the Spirit has found him first. It lives. It lives. It bleeds but it lives. And it has killed Derrick. I know him by his coat. It drags him here. Poor Derrick.

PART THREE

It must have been a terrible struggle. Poor me. It comes for me. I'm next. It has been roused and a spirit roused must be nothing nice. I'll fight back. I'll fight. Kill. Kill. Kill. Kill. I know what to do. Surprise. Surprise. Here it comes. My skin wants to hide in my bones.

(Hides. DERRICK *carries in* RIP.*)*

DERRICK: You are heavier than a goat because a goat I can carry far. I have to set you down for a while. Though here is not where I'd like to be. *(Sets him down)* So tell me—are you alive? I think you breathe but that maybe is the rain bouncing on your chest. I have a nice shack, when we get there you will be dry. Talk to me, I'd like some hot breath against my face.

SHEPHERD: *(From his hiding place)* Oh clever. Clever. The spirit has taken Derrick's voice. I know that voice, it has been stolen from him. It is a trick to get me. But I can play the trick too.

DERRICK: No? Then I will talk to you and that might loosen your tongue. Soon we will know everything about each other. It's nice to have a face in front of me even when I don't close my eyes.

SHEPHERD: *(Coming out of hiding)* Ho! Ho!

DERRICK: There you are, shepherd. I'd been calling. Two goats are loose in this rain.

SHEPHERD: They won't get far. I've been watching for the wolf. Remember the wolf?

DERRICK: Yes, I remember the wolf.

SHEPHERD: That body wears a nice coat. Just like Derrick's.

DERRICK: It is mine.

SHEPHERD: Of course. Of course. What one wins one keeps.

DERRICK: I found him down the way.

SHEPHERD: I know—you find them where you find them. It must have been a struggle. He was a strong man.

DERRICK: What are you talking about? There was no struggle. Though he moans, he doesn't move. I was about to tell him a story while we rested.

SHEPHERD: Is that your code to take off his head? When you say tell him a story, do you really mean take off his head? I've heard it said that instead of balls you people bowl heads.

DERRICK: Why are you talking like this?

SHEPHERD: You look like him too. How you people change shape.

DERRICK: Look, go find the goats. Go! go!

SHEPHERD: Can you breathe fire too? Or will I just drop dead because of your invisible hands?

DERRICK: Didn't you hear me? I told you to go! Go!

SHEPHERD: I'm going. I know that. I have no hope. As soon as I knew you were after me, I knew I must go.

DERRICK: Idiot, go! Get away from me. Why are you looking at me like that? Go!!

SHEPHERD: I'm going. But I will go like Derrick did. I will go screaming.

(Screams. He stabs DERRICK, who collapses.)

SHEPHERD: He bleeds. He bleeds. I did not expect this. I expected smoke to come out of his eyes and choke me. What do I do? What do I do? I'll get my brother, he'll know what to do.

(SHEPHERD runs out. DERRICK gasps. Long pause)

DERRICK: (To RIP) There is this story I wanted to tell you. Because I saw it in your face. There are stories in people's faces, Rip. See, I know who you are. I know

PART THREE

who you are. We have much in common. Listen.
(Cringes in pain) Once there were two brothers; the first was strong, handsome and wise; the second weak, ugly and stupid. One day the stupid brother was slicing an apple with his penknife and as his mind was not on what he was doing, his hand slipped and he cut off his finger. His wise brother used all of his wisdom trying to put the finger back on, but it just kept falling off. The stupid brother just cried and cried. Then something amazing happened, out of this finger grew first a whole hand, then an arm, then a chest, a body with legs, and finally a head and a face. So now the wise brother had two brothers, both weak, ugly and stupid. And he worked very hard to feed them both.
Months went by, until one day the three brothers were cutting wheat with a scythe. It was a hot day and one of the stupid brothers was not paying attention to what he was doing and his hand slipped and he cut off a finger. The wise brother felt terrible and used all of his wisdom trying to put the finger back on but it just kept falling off. Then suddenly from this finger grew another whole brother who was weak, ugly, and stupid.
This happened many more times until the wise brother had one hundred weak and ugly and stupid brothers all of which he had to feed. He worked and worked trying to feed his brothers, until he could not work anymore. Then the wise brother in his great wisdom got an idea. In the middle of the night he snuck away to the woods, took out his penknife and cut off his finger and set it on the ground and waited for it to grow a new body, one that would be handsome, strong and wise. He waited and waited. He became weak because of the blood rushing from his hand. And then he died. When the other brothers found him and saw the finger, they were amazed. And they said to each other: "Here all the time we thought our brother was

very wise, but only a stupid man would cut off his own finger."

(DERRICK *laughs. He becomes quiet. He sits. Leans over. He dies. Silence. Rain. The earth has become mud.* RIP *stirs. Slowly sits up.*)

RIP: Hurt. Hurt. The back. Like something's been biting the back. Ahhh! Hurt… Where am…? How long have I been here? What's this? (*To* DERRICK:) Get up! Get up! (*He struggles to get up.*) We got work. Got a crop to plant. Get up! (*Kicks* DERRICK) You. Get back into the fields. This is not time to… God, He gave us the strength to… (*Suddenly stares at* DERRICK.) You. You. No. No. I dream. Hurt. Gretchen. Gretchen!!!!!!!! (*Stumbles and falls. To* DERRICK) Fade. You are smoke. (*Pause. He looks around, unable to get up.*) Gretchen. Where is my wife who is my wife? I smell her on you, ghost. Has the rain washed away the world and uncovered you? Ahhhh! I hurt. I am thirsty. (*Opens his mouth and tries to drink the rain drops*) This will make me grow. (*Tries to drink*) Listen. (*Pause*) I hear. Listen. Gretchen, listen!!! You too, ghost. (*Pause*) Sing too. Sing too! Listen! (*He sings:*)
We gather together
To ask the Lord's blessing
He chastens and hastens
His will to make known.
Sing too!
So from the beginning
The fight we are winning
Sing… (*Short pause; then he collapses and dies.*)

Scene Seven

(*The hills. Mud. Dawn*)

(SHEPHERD *and his* BROTHER *enter.*)

PART THREE

SHEPHERD: Brother, look! There! There! One is Derrick and one is the spirit. The one who looks like Derrick is not Derrick because the spirit took his face. But see who has Derrick's coat—that is Derrick.

BROTHER: I see. It's been a bad night. I've seen a woman.

SHEPHERD: A woman! I saw her too! She's a spirit too.

BROTHER: A spirit?

SHEPHERD: Yes. Yes.

BROTHER: Good. Then I did right not to help. I knew there was some reason why I did not help.

SHEPHERD: Help how, brother?

BROTHER: I saw her on the cliff. She was looking down. So I looked down and there I saw something I had not seen. There was a wagon in the pass and suddenly part of this hill, because of the rain I suppose though maybe it was God, part of this hill it does slide down, it looked like a wall of mud, and it slides down and washes out the pass and this wagon is washed into the river and it sinks.

SHEPHERD: And? And?

BROTHER: And this woman who you say is a spirit...

SHEPHERD: I know. I know.

BROTHER: Who you know to be a spirit, she had been yelling like thunder itself, but when she sees this she screams like some thunder can scream and she falls on the ground. I get closer but not too close and I see that she is alive because in the mud I hear "gurgle, gurgle". And I listen, then it stops and it's like she drowned.

SHEPHERD: Drowned?

BROTHER: Yes. It's like she drowned.

SHEPHERD: In the mud?

BROTHER: Yes.

SHEPHERD: I didn't know one could drown in the mud.

BROTHER: I guess spirits can.

SHEPHERD: Yes, I guess they can. Now we know. Help me take Derrick back. The spirit I think we should burn.

BROTHER: Yes, let's burn the spirit.

(They start to drag off RIP *and* DERRICK.*)*

END OF PLAY

www.ingramcontent.com/pod-product-compliance
Lightning Source LLC
Chambersburg PA
CBHW061651040426
42446CB00010B/1680